MUSINGS OF AN INADEQUATE GOLFER

Malcolm Allen

TSL Publications

Contents

Dedication

To all the congenial golfing companions I have played with
over the years.
Keep at it – you'll crack it one day!

Golf Glossary

Golf has a vocabulary of its own. It is an international language which all golfers understand but one that non-golfers may find confusing. This glossary will make things crystal clear.

AGM	An annual opportunity to ask tricky questions which should have been presented to the committee in writing weeks ago.
Baseball cap	Headgear worn by golfers.
Bunker	An unnecessary addition to what is already an impossible game.
Bunker rake	A male member of a golf club who is also a cad. Also an agricultural implement always found far away from where it is needed.
Carvery	A prime cause of obesity.
Chief Executive	The Club Secretary (see also General Manager).
Club	A rod with a lump of metal at the end costing about £200.
Dessert trolley	A device which forces members to bend over so that they can breathe over the puddings.
Half mast (flag)	A signal to prospective members to get their application in.
Drying room	A source of second hand golf wear.
Fairway	A patch of green between groups of people searching for balls.
Flag marker or pin	An object to be returned to the hole by someone else.
General Manager	Club Secretary.
Given	A conceded putt which is accepted by slow players who then putt.
Golf Ball	42.7mm of frustration and despair. Something found but seldom bought.

Golf bag	A receptacle for dirty clothes, orange peel and stale peppermints.
Golf glove	An expensive and unnecessary accoutrement that hangs out of a hip pocket.
Golf lesson	A waste of money for most.
Golf Magazine	A publication which publishes the same material in every edition.
Golfing Society	Organised slow play.
Half-Way House	A refreshment stop which contravenes Rule 6-7, Undue Delay.
Head Groundsman	A trained professional who, according to the members, knows nothing.
Hole	108mm of frustration and despair. An object for slow players to peer into.
Juniors	Young golfers who play more slowly than the Seniors.
Kissing	A disgusting and unnecessary continental habit demonstrated at the end of a mixed foursome.
Ladies' Day	A marketing plan for the manufacturers of ear defenders.
Ladies	Women who play golf.
Men	Men who play golf.
Member	An expert on all golfing matters particularly agronomy.
Members' Club	An organisation run by a committee elected by the members who then criticise every decision made.
Men's Changing Room	A place of awful sights.
Mixed bar	A place avoided by male golfers.
Plus Fours	Very baggy trousers which fasten just below the knee. Also known as dysentery slacks.
Practice area	A place for perfecting faults.
Practice green	A green which has none of the characteristics of the course greens.
Practice	A waste of time for most.
Prestigious club	A place where a round of sandwiches costs £9.
Pro's Shop	An emporium of self-delusion.
Putter	A club designed to nudge the ball closer to the hole.

Range finder	An expensive gadget designed to hold up proceedings. It provides accurate distances to within one metre when the operator cannot judge a shot to within twenty metres.
Rough	Most of a golf course.
Rules	A subject for debate.
Seniors	Walking medical encyclopaedias.
Short rough	Longer grass which doesn't stop balls rolling into bunkers.
Silly Hat	Headgear which would normally be avoided by the wearer except on the golf course.
Silly trousers	See silly hat.
Slot machine	What?
Snooker room	A large space without a snooker table full of old people playing bridge.
Spike bar	A place with frayed carpets.
Starter	An official rarely seen around the course.
TV	A device hired in for the Open, the Masters and Rugby Internationals.
Swearing	A traditional and integral part of men's golf.
Tailored shorts	Clothing that male golfers should avoid.
The Professional	A deity; someone who can do no wrong.
The Assistant pro	A shop worker.
Wet weather gear	Uncomfortable clothing with unfindable pockets which delays play.
Winter Rules	Relief that some players take advantage of throughout the year.
Winter wheels	An enforced sale to boost the professional's turnover.
Yips	The name of every professional Korean woman golfer.

Fore

This book takes a tongue-in-cheek look at golf. Some of the language and terms used may appear unacceptable today but they are included as satirical observations of the past, present and indeed the future. No offence is meant and I hope that none is taken.

HOLE 1

'Expectations'

Par 4 Stroke Index 11

The Joy of Golf

It's competition day, the Monthly Medal or perhaps it's the Seniors rolling up at around midday to get in the way of a society, or it's the gathering of the clans on a Sunday morning when Waitrose or church don't beckon, work can be put on the backburner for another day and the kids are someone else's responsibility for a few hours. The gathering of the golf clan is a magical moment. The greetings from friends and acquaintances, the comments in the queue for coffee, anxious glances through the windows and reassuring comments about the weather or the not so reassuring from the Job's comforters, all add up to that festival of fun and fellowship which every golf club experiences most days of the week.

I say fellowship because this is the male experience. Whether it is the same for ladies I have no idea but if so it is not in the same way. My wife is appalled at the stories I tell her about the banter we men golfers have to accept. The derisory comments about each other's clothes, our appetites, our appearances even. No holds are barred and no mercy is expected. Would the ladies put up with this? I for one am not about to try it. Don't expect any mercy in the changing rooms either especially after a competition when the sights on display emerging from the showers are more akin to an audition for the *Horrors of Elm Street*.

Then it is the first tee. Those moments of anticipation when you know that the first strike will be straight, long and set the standard of the day are about to be trialled. But then the doubts creep in, you put away the driver and out with the three wood. Your friends hold their breath and that easy, smooth swing which you have practised in your mind for days evolves into an ugly lunge which deposits the ball a miserable forty yards forwards, beyond the ladies' tee perhaps, but in the rough. There is silence from your partner and a few derogatory remarks from your opponents and you're off on three and a half hours of joyous misery and unfettered determination.

Putting is the only stroke in any ball game that doesn't require even a small slice of athletic ability. The ball is standing still and so are you. All you have to do is pull (or push) the club back six inches or so and tap the ball into the hole. Of course length and direction come into this but you have been pretty successful on the practice green, the carpet and in your mind's eye. You can even recall your own mother, bless her, in her hat, floral dress and cardigan knocking the ball over the bridge and through the windmill on the Magic Putting Green at Bournemouth so many years ago. But it is not like that at all, is it? Whether relaxed or rigid, fat or thin grip, hands apart or together, over or under you are forever reminded of the little girl saying as her father putted, 'why won't the little ball go into the little hole, Daddy?' Why? Can no one write a book called *How to hole that fourth vital putt?*

What an arena we are fortunate to enjoy as well. Very few golf courses are ugly and many of them are simply magnificent. My course is famous for its deer and woodpeckers and most others have a signature hole or two featuring water or special trees and bushes. Views of mountains and sea, I suppose, are the most memorable but our own course always will seem near the top. Nevertheless, it is the company that makes the round so enjoyable. Whether it be total strangers whom you are drawn with in a competition or a few mates who arrange a four ball together, the craic, as the Irish say, the conversation, the encouragement, the good sportsmanship and, yes, even the derisive comments cannot be surpassed by any other sport, and I've played most. What other game as well enables you to be competitive with much younger people who are physically more able? Is there another pursuit that you can continue to play into your dotage and what other sport allows you to compare your performance against the top players? Your 88 can be seen against Tiger's 65 even though he was playing from the back tees and the greens were twice as fast.

The eighteenth is completed and sadly the game is over and the reality of your inability to 'crack it' creeps in. Sure, you had a birdie but you missed the chance of another and double bogeyed at least three you should have bogeyed. The only hole you will report of course is the birdie and that conversation will soon be forgotten in the good comradeship and laughter of the 19th. Sometimes it's just a beer, at other times it is a three course lunch with wine and for the Seniors a cup of tea and a tea cake bought by the losers.

Then slightly stiff and with a sore back it is off home with your mind already set on the next time when you will most certainly break 80, or 85 or 90! Does it matter? Of course it does. Perhaps that new driver the Pro recommends would help after all!

HOLE 2

'The Great Valley'

Par 5 Stroke Index 7

Keep Your Head Down

I sat on my camp stool gazing out at the splendour of the Spin Ghar mountains which dominated the view north and south. The smoke and aroma of my first cigar of the day hung around my head. A turbaned mess servant flitted silently to my side. 'Would you like another dram, Major McDonald?' and he proffered the tray that was already charged with my favourite malt.

'Aye,' I thought, 'it's not the same as a dram in the Highlands with the wintry sun rising o'er the Grampians near Lochaber but it's not bad all the same.'

Behind me I listened to the comforting sounds of the few officers still taking breakfast in our field mess. It was a tented affair as was right for a battalion on operations in dangerous country in the 1870s but it was comfortable and well furnished; certainly well worth the loss in transit of a few dozen or so oxen and labourers who had carried it on the long trek up through the Sindh.

'Ah well, it is a soldier's lot to make sacrifices when called to the Queen's duty,' I thought, 'and any bloody fool can be uncomfortable, if they want.'

There was fizz and ping and a bullet sped close by my head, smashing into a portrait of a previous Colonel of the 71st Highland Light Infantry. 'Bloody Afridis,' I snorted, 'couldn't hit an elephant's arse with a handful of gravel.'

Just then Lt Sandy Hook-Ballantyne appeared holding a cup of Camp coffee. 'Good breakfast then, Sandy?' I asked, 'And are you ready for the match?'

'Spot on, Donald, on both counts, and I'm looking forward to a hard fought game as well.' He paused for a moment, picked up the Enfield Musketoon that was always kept handily loaded on the veranda and took a pot shot at something moving on a cliff face opposite. There was a cry and a turbaned Afghan tumbled to the rocks below. 'Cracking shot,' I commented and reflected on the first time I'd met Sandy.

A couple of years ago I was with a group of officers sampling a chotapeg or two with the Colonel in the club in Peshawar when a fresh faced young subaltern approached and saluted.

'Lt Sandy Hook-Ballantyne reporting for duty, sir.'

'Ah, you're very welcome, young Ballantyne,' said the Colonel, 'pull up a chair and join us.'

'Actually, sir,' said the young man in a slightly sniffy way, 'the name is Hook-Ballantyne.'

The Colonel sat back in his chair, allowed his monocle to fall from his eye and replied, 'In which case you'd better draw up two bloody chairs.'

But, from this inauspicious start, young Sandy had proven himself and this morning I would take him on in the final of the Waterloo Cup, the rather grandiosely named regimental golf competition which, today, would be played on the little six-holer we had carved out of the inhospitable terrain that we were defending. Just then, Sgt Mackenzie stamped to attention on the path leading to the mess.

'Escort ready and briefed, sir, and the bearers are on the tee with your clubs. You have a new bearer, Major McDonald. Akbar was shot dead while cleaning your clubs in the stream. We recovered them, sir, and dried them off.' I was much relieved. I had bought a new spoon and would have hated to have lost it in the fast flowing water.

Thus, accompanied by our escort and in high spirits we made our way to the first tee where our bearers were sheltering behind a rock in a cowardly fashion but they stood up as we approached and handed us our drivers. Sgt Mackenzie ordered the escort to fan out and take up positions covering the surrounding terrain. I noticed a few kitehawks hovering over the bank of the stream where Akbar lay. I hoped someone would remove the corpse shortly otherwise there would be an unholy mess around for a couple of days.

The first hole was a neat little par four with a dogleg and, having won the toss, I drove first, hitting a bit of a fade but it was acceptable. Sandy always preferred a brassie and he hit a long high draw which landed just off the fairway. Two forecaddies ran out to mark the balls dodging and weaving as the damned Afridis opened up with their Jezails from long range. Our escort returned fire and silence ensued. When I reached my ball I noticed my forecaddie was bleeding profusely from a wound to his head and I had to order him not to moan during my backswing. Nevertheless, I hit a very nice mashie and the gutty flew high and long in the mountain air and fell onto the first green. Well, it was called a green but it was actually a mixture of sand and compressed oxen dung, but pretty good really. It did attract the flies however but we had a man with a swat on hand to help while we were considering our putts. Sandy also hit a good shot and we both had two putts before moving to the second hole. In the meantime the escort redeployed but with one Highlander missing. 'Not too serious,' we were informed by the Sergeant. 'The doctor thinks he can save the arm. 'Jolly good,' I nodded.

We both played niblicks to the short par three second which was close to the edge of a ravine. I hit my ball a shade too firmly and it just rolled over the edge onto a ledge about five feet below. These gutties are quite expensive you know, so I ordered the forecaddie over the edge. He nimbly obliged, threw the ball back to me and stupidly lost his footing on the climb back up and fell sixty or seventy feet into the river below. We couldn't see whether he survived but it was a bloody nuisance to lose a forecaddie so early in the game and I was loath to deplete the escort in such a cause. We just had to get on with it and being British we did. Sandy went one-up here because of my penalty shot.

We played the third exceedingly badly, both of us mis-hitting our drives and failing to get up in four and then I was stymied. A good shot with the jigger restored the situation for a minute but Sandy is a fine putter and holed out from three feet. We laughed when a dud shell from one of the Afghans' ancient cannon fizzed and buzzed around our feet before we made our way to the halfway house or, rather, a lone tree that provided a bit of shade. The mess staff had set up a table with a crisp white cloth hanging to the ground and cold beers in an ice bucket. I was somewhat annoyed that the waiter was absent but then I noticed him crouching behind the tree rather than standing attentively to attention ready to pour our drinks. 'Beer wallah,' I called. 'What the hell are you on? You know the form, so attend to your duties or it's demotion to latrine wallah for you.' He smiled nervously and, somewhat reluctantly and with a shaking hand poured our drinks. A single rifle shot sounded and he flinched. We didn't.

Just then, with a terrible scream a figure emerged from under the table. It was a Pathan woman brandishing a traditional sword of the Barakzais sect. Pathan women are not simply mothers and wives as are our fragrant memsahibs. They are fierce defenders of their territory and God help any Tommy or Jock who would fall into their hands. They were adept at slicing off the eyelids of prisoners, covering the eyes in honey and burying the unfortunate prisoner up to his neck so that ants had free range to feast on the honey and the delicious eyeballs. That was not the only thing they were good at slicing off either.

With contorted face this ghastly creature hurled herself at me but luckily I was carrying my cleek ready for the next tee. Keeping a straight left arm and making a full shoulder turn I swung the club and gave her a sharp crack on the ankle. She tumbled to the ground whimpering in agony. 'Goodness,' said young Sandy, 'will women never understand the etiquette of this game. I believe as well that she was shouting "get in the hole" in Pashtun?' We laughed over our beer as she limped away. I'm afraid my cleek was now useless as the hickory shaft had broken in half with the force of the blow.

The fourth was not a long hole but still a testing par four. I drove with my spoon as did Sandy and I played my second shot to the green with a niblick. The gutty soared high into the air but then there was a shout. Sgt Mackenzie came running wildly up the fairway screaming, 'Go back, gentlemen, go back, an ambush party is hiding in the wadi.' And then a bullet struck him in the back of the head and he crashed face down in the dust, his kilt riding up his back with the force of the fall. Fortunately Cpl McIver, the second in command of the escort, rallied what was left of it and made a determined bayonet charge on the filthy natives hiding in the wadi. What a fine sight it was as the Jocks ran like devils towards the enemy, kilts swinging and their bonnets at a jaunty angle. As they ran they screamed the regimental battle cry and Sandy and I joined in as we watched. I felt immensely proud to be part of this great regiment. In no time the cold steel won the day and those Afghans who could run, did. Our brave marksmen had good sport picking them off as they retreated into the hills. Two or three of the Jocks lay still on the barren plain but what a splendid place to die for your country!

There was nothing more we could do for Sgt Mackenzie but there was a problem. My high approach shot had fallen short of the green and was now resting on the deceased. Worse, as we could observe from his displaced kilt it had come to rest between the skinny cheeks of his buttocks. Sandy and I conferred and neither of us could think of a rule for relief that would apply. Sgt Mackenzie could not be considered as GUR thus we determined that the ball must be played as it lay. So, taking my jigger I played a firm pitch towards the green ensuring that I reduced the divot to a minimum out of respect for the cadaver. Of course, as a result, I got no back spin leaving myself a long putt which I missed. Sandy missed his as well but it was hardly surprising as the green was in a sorry state after the escort had charged over it. I was still one down and the escort about eight. I called Cpl McIver over and gave him a well-deserved dressing down. 'If you have to make another assault on the course make sure your chaps run around the green and not across it. Look, McIver, it's an absolute bloody ruin.' He took it in good heart and limped back to his section.

Apart from a few stray rounds passing overhead there was a period of relative calm as we played the fifth, a long par four with an uphill approach to the green. Sandy made an uncharacteristic error on his approach leaving the ball well short whereas I hit a corker with my second. Sandy conceded the hole and all square we moved to the last. Our escort by this time was quite thin on the ground and the remaining forecaddie had deserted. These people had no intestinal fortitude.

The last was a very tricky par three, not long but well-guarded by bunkers and an overhanging rock formation. I took a baffy and Sandy a mid-iron and we both made the green. As we strolled forward discussing the latest rumours of Angela Westbrook's rather scandalous behaviour we were blown to our knees by the most tremendous explosion which was shortly followed by a storm of debris falling from the sky. We looked back and saw a pall of smoke hanging over the Regiment's encampment. 'Goodness gracious, I think the magazine has gone up,' suggested Sandy, 'I hope my ponies are all right as it is damn close to the stables.' As President of the Mess Committee I was more concerned about the mess silver. But what could we do?

The green was a total disaster covered in bits and pieces, far too much really to clear the line of putt. An object was also partially obscuring the hole which on closer inspection was revealed as a severed hand. 'Not one of our chaps I believe,' observed Sandy, 'and I don't think we can move it as it doesn't fall under the definition of a Loose Impediment.' I agreed and suggested that in the circumstances we call it a day and halve the match. 'Will you shake on that?' I asked. We looked at the hand obscuring the hole and walked off arm in arm laughing at the irony of this remark. Of course we had to carry our clubs as both bearers had buggered off.

That evening's Regimental Dinner Night was special. Some of our colleagues were missing, or missing bits, and the mess looked somewhat the worse for wear as a result of its proximity to the explosion. Still, the candlelight gleamed on what remained of the silver and our glasses were rapidly filled and heartily emptied. After the loyal toast and five or six circulations of the port, the Colonel, whose leg had been blown off by the explosion, propped himself up and delivered a simple but rousing finale to the celebration.

'Today has seen another glorious chapter in the history of the Regiment and a fine example of the tenacity and valour of the officers who lead it. Never before has the Waterloo Cup been contested in such strenuous circumstances and never before has the result been a tie, an honourable one I am sure you will agree. I, for one, am glad there were no losers on this day so let me give you the winners of the Khyber Cup, for that is what it will be known as in future, Major McDonald and Lieutenant Ballantyne, er,' and he looked up with a twinkle in his monocled eye, 'Hook-Ballantyne I believe.'

That was the last time the cup was played for as the next day the Regiment entered the Khyber Pass to clear it of the marauding Afghans once and for all. Unfortunately our game that day was not up to par and I was the only survivor. Years later, as I sit in the evening sun gazing out over the rugged Grampians, the bent and battered Khyber Cup on a table by my side, I think of that wondrous time and the officers and men with whom I had the privilege to serve. With my remaining arm I raised my glass. 'To golf, Sandy and the 71st.' What glorious memories.

HOLE 3

'Soon'

Par 3 Stroke Index 15

Golf in the Next Century

The year 2149 was a great year for British Golf. Our top player Citizen 118 (*) code (A) won the Open Championship on the wonderful Territory 7 course with an incredible four round score of 138 and he then went on to win the Virtual Masters in the Albert Hall by a similar total. Four million competitors took part in this wonderful event which was screened throughout the world but, sadly, not in Territory 7 because the Territory Broadcasting Corporation (TBC) had failed to bid for the concession as it had spent all its E-dollars on a new historical drama series entitled *The Last English Monarch*.

Golf in 2149 is very different to what it was a hundred or so years ago. For a start it is not run by the R&A and the USGA although the latter still holds sway in some districts of Americana. Of course, many years ago Britain became part of F-GREST, that is the Federation of Germany and the Remainder of the European Socialist Territories and is now called Territory 7. This event is proudly symbolised on our national flag by a black T7 on a yellow background with a map of what was England, Ireland, Scotland, Wales and Iceland outlined in green. The flag of course is changed annually on Federation Day (25th December) when the relative sizes of the countries are amended so that any one does not appear superior to another.

Golfers are, today, far bigger and stronger. The average height of a citizen is around 1.98 metres and this in itself means that the ball is propelled much further than in the past even though it has been modified. Under F-GREST legislation there is no differential between males and females who participate in competitions on an equal footing. As the

President of the F-GREST PGA, Citizen 319 (**) code (ZL) proclaimed, 'All citizens are equal regardless of colour, sex or mutation.'

There is a demographic difference as well. Our population has grown to well over 124 million and this has resulted in an extreme shortage of open spaces even though houses have been replaced by small Accommodation Pods for unlicensed (Single) citizens and Domestic Pods for licensed (Officially Recognised Co-habitants) citizens. In fact only one per cent of the Territory is classified as green space, the remainder being taken up by Pods (21 per cent), entertainment facilities (3 per cent), transport and terminal facilities (10 per cent), Amazon warehouses (32 per cent), and the remainder by correctional facilities and on-shore wind farms.

Happily, the traditional club has survived though. Take Sunningdale, for example. It lies in the 121st Urban Conurbation of Wandsworth and Basingstoke, sub-department 10 (Bagshot). The traditional clubhouse pod complete with a Bonsai replica of its trade mark oak tree is set in the centre of a magnificent six-hole, astro-turf complex including silicon powder bunkers as sand has been banned by the F-GREST Parliament; an abrasive damage threat to the eyes apparently. Playing there is a great experience as the Urban Conurbation Leisure Council, which runs the course, have come up with a unique system to maintain the traditions of our great game by placing huge screens along each fairway which shield the players from the monotonous views of high level accommodation pods and the East Windlesham refugee camps which surround the course. These camps are populated mainly by impoverished Scottish refugees making their way south for a better life after oil ran out and whiskey was banned by F-GREST on ecological and social grounds. The screens are cleverly programmed to feature views of Sunningdale in bygone years or, indeed, any of the other classic courses of the last century if required.

Alongside each fairway is a constantly moving walkway which transports players to their ball after they have played their shot. Just step on and off at will. Music, video and Wi-Fi connections are available throughout its length. As this is an egalitarian game there are no individual clubs or balls, simply a selection on each tee which can be chosen from a dispenser using an App on your Personal Communication Device (PCD). The cost of maintenance and replacement is covered by the fees. Scores are also recorded automatically so there is no chance of cheating. To compensate for the Territory-wide reduction in the bird and other wildlife populations caused mainly by the wind farms and building development, bird song is played over speakers and, often to the amazement of younger players, robotic animals such as very rare rabbits and squirrels are located at suitable sites around the course mischievously peeping out from the carefully planted artificial flora.

It is understandable that membership of such a prestigious course as Sunningdale is in huge demand so the committee has restricted full membership to 15,000 which is comfortably catered for by an efficient 24 hour operating cycle aided by virtual sunlight (VS). Leisure pursuits are in high demand in 2149 as automation means that very few people work in the traditional way. The exceptions are lawyers, undertakers and politicians. Access to the club is easy too as the Sunning Hydrogen Intercity Transit terminal is close by on the site of the former Ladies' course easily ensuring that players can enjoy a sociable 20 minutes in the quaintly named 19th hole before departing to their pods. After a hard fought game it is wonderful to sit in the comfortable rows of stools with built-in headphones listening to the clicks and peeps as members enjoy the recollections of their game over their PCDs. What could be better?

Sunningdale still caters for a few Societies but only official government ones and what a wonderful package is available. For as little as 20 E-dollars players can enjoy two rounds of golf, refreshments from the snack machine room on arrival and a wonderful three course lunch convivially shared around the Bruce Critchley Nutrient Dispenser. A huge range of healthy and delicious pills are available, washed down by a carton or two of Sunningdale's specially selected wines piped directly from the world renowned blending facility in Staines.

The world has undoubtedly changed but, thank God, the glorious game of golf is still with us in all its glory. Hang on, 'God', oh no. Can't say that. 'The 'illustrious being or conscience or whatever you believe' – that's what I meant.

HOLE 4

'Hope'

Par 4 Stroke Index 1

Hints for Hackers

Every golf magazine carries illustrated articles with titles like *How to hit the perfect drive* or *Make the pitching wedge work for you*. They are written by some youthful professional or golfing guru and they hoodwink the average hacker into thinking that s/he can do the same. Let's get it right from the start – you can't and you never will. 'Why is that?' you may ask, and here is the answer. You are not young, supple or talented and you seldom practise properly. In fact you are a pretty useless golfer. Thus, it is far better if you hone your own style working to the adage that there are many ways of skinning a cat. So, for the high handicap hacker with a 46 inch plus waist and the athletic ability of a Chelsea Pensioner with haemorrhoids, pay close attention to the following.

The Drive
The aim is to ensure the ball travels forwards and, if you are male, beyond the ladies' tee. Take a stance with more than half your weight on the back foot (we will assume you are right-handed) and the club held firmly with some form of grip. Harry Vardon developed his own so why can't you? The ball should be teed high in the middle of the stance where there is some likelihood of you being able to reach it. The club should be taken away inside out, or outside in, it doesn't matter in your case, until you reach the maximum turn of your shoulders. With an exaggerated wrist cock this should present the club at the completion of the back swing at a little more than parallel to the ground pointing away from the hole. Now, in order to generate some power through the shot, you should be thinking 'whoosh,' so, the moment you reach the apogee of your take

away, or preferably slightly before, thrash the club towards the position where you last remember seeing the ball.

The follow through is most important and depends entirely on weight transference during the strike. It is best to leave most weight on the rear (right) foot at contact while at the same time lifting onto the toes and pivoting so that at the conclusion of the shot the 'at ease' position is adopted with the shoulders at right angles to the intended flight of the ball. As the ball has now left the club, balance is immaterial so continue the movement as you will.

The Fairway Wood or Iron

Where possible and regardless of winter rules, nudge the ball into a better lie, as high as possible. The shot should be played within the same principles as the drive but with a couple of minor changes. As the ball is not teed your prime thought process is to restrict topping it. Thus the hacker must attempt to hit down on the ball with a hooded face and reduce the follow through to knee height. This demands a stiff arm and no wrist action. Care must be taken not to strike the ground in front of the ball as this can seriously damage wrist tendons or, worse, cause a rupture.

The Approach Shot

This should be the third or fourth shot of the hole, particularly on a par three, but it may not be. A short iron or pitching wedge is needed. A stance should be adopted whereby the ball is positioned opposite the left foot which should be splayed out to the left. The right foot should be slightly forward allowing the stance to open and the right knee flexed and bent inwards. This generates a peculiar but solid, crab-like stance which restricts the back swing almost entirely.

The club should be taken back slowly with the blade open to enhance the desired spooning or lifting action and then returned to the ball with a violent thrusting jab accompanied by a collapse of the right leg and hip. An expletive is always helpful at this stage.

The importance of opening the face of the club cannot be emphasised enough. Sometimes the ball may rise in the air and, undoubtedly, fall somewhat short of the hole, or the green or in the bunker but if the shot is made imperfectly the blade of the club will at least impact halfway up the ball, propelling it at ground level in the general direction of the target. Modern club design ensures that the ball will usually travel over the ground at least as far as it will through the air.

The Bunker Shot

Don't even try is my advice, simply pick up. But, if you must ... firstly, take care entering and especially leaving the bunker. It is the right etiquette to enter and leave at the lowest point but in your case that is the wisest way too. It is unlikely that the ball is plugged as that would require your approach to have reached the bunker in full flight but if it is, it won't be when you play your next shot. Take a sand wedge and address the ball with an open stance with the ball back opposite the right foot. Make a long back swing, out to in, allowing the blade of the club to strike the sand two inches behind the ball (when coming back down that is!). While still accelerating the club make a full follow through. When the sand has cleared, try again. Remember also to rake the bunker when you leave because, without doubt, you will have done immense damage to it.

The Putt

After studying the line of the putt and beating the soles of your shoes with the putter as you have seen the professionals do, executing the stroke is easy as no athletic ability is required at all. The main thing is to strike the ball firmly but decelerating the club head as you do so. Remember, 'three putts' is good!

Conclusion

Knowing that you are never going to get better just enjoy the scenery, your playing partners and the lunch. Mind you, if you really are desperate, an eleven can easily be changed to a four on the scorecard!

HOLE 5

'Be Watchful'

Par 5 Stroke Index 5

Letters to the Captain

The role of Captain of a Golf Club is one of the most onerous offices that a sensible chap (or chapess) can be persuaded to accept. He is the focal point for all criticism, complaint and dissent and he must lead with a reasoned smile, a forever-open ear, and deep pockets. His situation is made worse by modern communication methods, particularly Email, which allows unwarranted access at all hours of the day to his personal attention. Some correspondence is helpful but by no means all.

Dear Captain,

I am extremely grateful for the thought that the committee has put into the rules for the wearing of shorts by gentlemen players. I agree whole-heartedly that they must be tailored, have no external pockets, buttons or thongs hanging off them like the buckskin breeches favoured by Red Indians in the Wild West, and that they must be knee-length. I also agree that shorts should be worn with long socks and that those rather effeminate looking ankle socks are banned.

However, not all can be said to be correct and by that I refer to the naked leg exhibited in the gap between the bottom of the shorts and the top of the sock. Some members, I have noticed, are not as careful about the tailoring as they should be thus exposing too great an expanse of knee and the flesh above and below it. The results are some extraordinar-ily grotesque sights. I suggest that the rules should be extended to say exactly how far above the kneecap shorts should extend and, similarly, how far below the kneecap the sock roll should begin. A rule of thumb could be introduced whereby the length of a box of Bryant and Mays matches held at the centre of the patella could indicate the required length.

I personally never wear shorts because I have thoughts for the feelings of others. The exception is on holiday when I wear my old Army khaki drill shorts. If Johnny Foreigner doesn't like it he can lump it I say. The fact is that even the most tailored of shorts and carefully rolled socks will not disguise the truly awful appearance of some gentlemen's knees. I appreciate that many 'owners' never see them in all their glory because they are in the dead ground under their stomachs but, in my opinion, some are so hideous that their owners should employ a man with a red flag to walk in front of them to warn the lady members.

Thus, Captain, I suggest that as well as tightening the rules, you ask all gentlemen members who wish to wear shorts to examine their legs, and their consciences, before inflicting their vanity on others.

Yours sincerely
Digby Patterson (Lt Col ret'd)

Dear Digby,
Thank you for your comments on the wearing of shorts. The committee has considered your suggestions but feel that a further strengthening of the rules would be difficult to enforce. You will appreciate as well that criticism of a fellow member's appearance, no matter how well intentioned, could cause offence. I agree that at times we all need to look at ourselves and see us as others do.

Yours sincerely
John Adams, Captain

Dear Captain,
I have noticed a small hole in the carpet near the front door of the clubhouse. It is not big at the moment but is worth fixing. I thought that I would bring it to your attention, a stitch in time and all that, you know.

Regards
Jimmy Pelle-Buxton

Dear Captain,

I was astonished to hear that the ground staff are to introduce French drains to the course. Worse, I understand that the construction will begin on St George's Day. Could you please ensure that they are renamed British drains. What next, bidets?

Yours sincerely

Digby Patterson (Lt Col Ret'd)

Dear Digby,

I admire your patriotism but French drains have nothing to do with France. They are in fact the invention of Henry French, a 19th century judge and farmer who used them extensively on his own land. French is quite a common name stemming from its Norman and Irish origins. May I also point out that we buy all our vegetables, including Brussels sprouts from local farmers.

Yours respectfully

John Adams, Captain.

Dear Captain,

I would like to bring to your attention the sorry standard of sandwiches in the club. While the rest of the food in the dining room is of a high quality I have to say that the standard of sandwich is not. Yes, you get what you ask for whether it be tuna, cheddar or prawn but that's it. A little celery or mayonnaise in the tuna would make all the difference. A simple lettuce leaf and a slice of tomato with the cheddar would count for a lot, even a little pickle or relish would help but no, it's plain what you ordered and that's it. This club is worth garnish and pickle, Captain, so can we have some?

Yours sincerely

Fred Anderson

Dear Fred,

I am eternally grateful to you for bringing to my attention your view of the standard of sandwich in our club. As you know, John Montague, the 4th Earl of Sandwich invented this form of nourishment when ordering meat between two slices of bread to avoid the interruption of a proper meal when playing cards. Additionally he preferred no butter, no relish, no pickle, just plain bread and meat and for the very good reason that he didn't want sticky fingers when playing cards. I am tempted to add that

we are a traditional club and there is a strong argument in saying that what was good enough for the 4th Earl of Sandwich is good enough for us. Instead I have asked the catering staff to offer extra relish and supplements at a small additional cost. I trust this move will satisfy your epicurean demands. However, as I have said, the good Earl was keen to ensure that his grip on the cards was not impaired as a result of his eating habits. Perhaps I should draw your attention to the Rules of Golf Rule 14-3 which bans any device or unusual equipment that might assist in gripping the club. Tomato sauce, I believe, can be quite a useful adhesive in wet weather. So, be careful.
Yours sincerely
John Adams
The Captain

Dear Captain,
I have recently noticed that two bidets have been installed in the gentlemen's changing rooms. I know that they are carefully screened but can I remind you that bidets are like Company Chairmen – they are there, they look good, but nobody is sure what useful purpose they serve. Have we nothing better to do with our annual subscriptions?
Yours sincerely
Digby Patterson (Lt Col Ret'd)

Dear Digby,
The decision to provide bidets received the support of the whole committee as part of the refurbishment of the changing rooms and the cost was negligible in comparison to the total bill for this necessary project. I accept that you personally don't approve of the installation but others are in favour and they object to you using the bidets to clean your golf clubs. I would ask you to desist.
J Adams, Captain

Dear Captain,
I don't seem to have had a reply to my letter about the hole in the carpet as yet. The memsahib has noticed it as well and is concerned that it might catch a high heel. I'll leave it up to you, old chap.
Jimmy Pelle-Buxton

Dear Captain,

I see that the Lady Captain has nominated the bunker in front of the short seventh hole as her Charity. All who fall foul of it must subscribe to a collecting box in the bar. This may be a noble idea but is this not discrimination against the gentlemen players? After all, the ladies start 30 yards nearer the hole and from an easier direction.

Yours sincerely

Digby Patterson (Lt Col Ret'd)

Dear Colonel,

This is not a permanent addition to the club's activities and the Charity is a worthwhile one. You are reminded that the donations are purely voluntary as were those for the renovation appeal for the NAAFI Memorial in Hounslow which you initiated last year.

Yours

Mr J Adams, Captain

Dear Captain,

I have raised the issue of the lighting system in the gentlemen's changing room before. It appears to go on and off at random intervals but I am assured that there is nothing random about it at all. Apparently it is controlled by a 'motion sensor.' As I explained at the time this is all very well for the younger, more active members of our club but for we seniors, who tend to move in a more deliberate way, the occasional lapses into darkness can be disconcerting. However, not anything to worry about, until now.

About four weeks ago I drove to the club for a bit of practice and it was on a Thursday which is Ladies' Day. This was apparent by the paucity of gentlemen around. I made my way first to the professional's shop to draw my ball tokens and before returning to the practice area I diverted into the changing rooms. The lights were off but, to give the system its due, they clicked on as I entered and I took advantage of the illumination to read the notices. Then I decided to repair to one of the cubicles for a period of quiet contemplation. Captain, I had hardly been ensconced for more than a few minutes when all the lights went out and I was plunged into the blackness of the tomb.

It was not a pleasant experience and my heart beat faster than it has done in years. A sense of panic began to overtake me but, fortunately, my military training soon clicked in and I regained control. Realising that light depended on movement I windmilled my arms and legs furiously, a difficult thing to do in the position that I was in which I'm sure you will appreciate, but to no avail and the Stygian gloom continued. So I thought again.

Fumbling in the dark I located the toilet roll and unhooked it from its container and then, pausing only long enough to mentally calculate the trajectory required to clear the intervening partition, I hurled it as hard as I could in the direction of the outer chamber hoping that its velocity would be detected by the sensor and that I would be reunited with a source of light. Nothing happened.

Two thoughts crossed my mind at this time. First, in no sense of the word could this device be described as a motion sensor and, second, my precipitate action had changed what had been an unfortunate situation into a somewhat unhygienic one. There was only one thing for it, Captain, with my trousers around my ankles I exited the cubicle in that ungainly sideways and bent-kneed crouch so favoured by low-arsed Samurai warriors, and the lights came on.

And then, a gentleman appeared. He was not a member. From my lowly position I looked up at him with a weak smile on my face and he peered down at me with an expression which can only be described as a mixture of disbelief and disgust. He then turned on his heel and left. I retrieved the toilet roll and continued with my ablutions.

I am pleased to report, Captain, that I have suffered no long term ill-effects from this experience but I am one of the more robust members of the Seniors' Section and if this situation had involved one of our more delicately framed colleagues, what was a rather unedifying experience could have turned into a calamity.

I therefore ask the Committee to review the lighting system in the gentlemen's changing rooms with less of an eye on energy efficiency and more to health and safety.
Yours faithfully
Sir William Price (Colonel, Ret'd)

Dear Sir William,
The committee regrets the inconvenience that the lighting system caused you but have decided that to replace the current system would be too expensive. Although appreciating your point about the slower movement of Seniors, it was considered exceptional if there was only one Senior alone in the changing rooms for any length of time and that 'synergy' so

to speak would keep the lights burning. However, a hand torch will be placed in each cubicle from now on just in case. I should add that spare toilet rolls are stored on the handles of the lavatory brushes to the left of the pan.

Yours sincerely

The Captain

Dear Captain,

A cry in the wilderness or perhaps my email thing isn't working properly but the hole in the carpet near the door is now fraying at the edges. Awfully unsightly I think.

Jimmy Pelle-Buxton

Dear Jimmy,

Thank you for bringing to my attention the hole in the carpet near the front door. I apologise for not replying earlier but this matter was not at the top of our priorities ever since the trolley shed burned down, severely injuring the starter and destroying 60% of the clubs therein. All of them brand new according to their owners. Of course, repairing a carpet is not the easiest thing to do so we have decided to mark it with a white line in the same fashion that we mark Ground Under Repair. The prime aim of this is to ensure that no lady or gentleman inadvertently trips as a result of the hole until such time as a repair can be effected. However, we have also decided on a local rule that in the unlikely event of a ball in play landing within the Carpet Under Repair (CUR) zone a player will be entitled to a free drop in a dropping zone just outside the french windows in the bar. We have decided to dispense with 'The nearest point of relief' edict under rule 20 as it was agreed that a member's back swing would be seriously impeded by the adjacent flower decoration and the umbrella stand. I am sure that you will agree that this is a sensible course of action.

Yours sincerely

The Captain

Dear Captain,

At the special meeting called last week to discuss Governance we were made aware of the need to ensure absolute equality between the gentle-

man and lady members of our club. Such things as use of public rooms, playing conditions, tee times and reserved days. I am all in favour of this as long as it does not involve end of game etiquette. The men shake hands and the ladies kiss each other. May that status quo remain.
Yours sincerely
D Patterson MBE Lt Col (Ret'd)

Dear Lieutenant Colonel Patterson,
The status quo will be maintained. You are reminded to keep your dog on a lead.
The Captain

Dear Captain,
I am loath to report this but Squadron Leader Harrison shamelessly farts in the public rooms. For all I know he may have a persistent medical condition like Idiopathic Steatorrhia but what I and other members find appalling is that he accepts no responsibility for the transgression and blames it on his dog, Max.
Yours concernedly
Benjamin Swag

Dear Benjamin,
You are not the first to have noticed this but I believe this problem was resolved last week by Admiral Washout. When Squadron Leader Harrison unjustly blamed Max for an unusually loud and foul eruption of intestinal gas and ordered him outside, the Admiral agreed and told Max 'to get out before your owner shits all over you.' I believe the gallant aviator took note of this.
Yours sincerely
John

Dear Captain,
I have copied this letter to the Lady Captain. As a lady member for a number of years I was most interested in the views expressed on equality at the Governance meeting the other day. A situation that irks a number of us ladies concerns the on course 'rest room' facilities. There are none. This is all very well for the gentlemen players who can, and often do, depart to the woods at frequent intervals, not always to look for a ball.

We ladies, on the other hand, either have to 'hold on' or make a run for it and neither option is good for our game. May I suggest, therefore, that some form of rest room facility be installed at the far end of the course. Nothing exotic by any means, but comfortable, secure and in keeping with the natural beauty of our lovely course. I'm sure that you can think of something.
Yours sincerely
Dorothy Larkin

Dear Captain,
I received a copy of Dorothy's letter to you about a rest room facility on the course for ladies. What nonsense. I spent many years in the Royal Air Force and only the basic facilities were provided. In the field you put up with what the men had to put up with. A rest room at the extremity of the course could never merge into the background and would, anyway, be vandalised soon enough. And who would maintain it? An absolute non-starter so ignore the request. I will deal with the girl.
Anthea Netherstay (Wing Commander Ret'd)

Dear Anthea,
Wizard prang, good show, I'll leave it to you.
Yours sincerely
John Adams, Captain

Dear Captain
The room reserved as the overflow gentlemen's changing room is seldom used as such. Might I suggest that it could be converted at very little cost into a sauna room. Not only would this provide a splendid new facility for the club but it would be medically beneficial for members with aches and pains. It would have to be open to both lady and gentlemen players and I suggest that a rota could be easily maintained if use was tied in with competition days. Ladies could have sole use on Ladies' Days and competitions and the same for Gentlemen and Seniors. Mixed competitions could be a problem but I am sure that the committee could come up with a solution. Just a thought, though.
Yours sincerely
Roderick Penneston-House

Dear Captain

What a splendid idea about a sauna. Roddy is such a forward thinker. As for worrying about mixed saunas I shouldn't lose any sleep over that. As we girls used to say in the RAF, 'If you see something that you have never seen before then shoot it!'

Yours enthusiastically

Anthea Netherstay (Wing Commander Ret'd)

Dear Captain,

I think I saw a cockroach in the dining room. What a disgrace so please do something about it.

Yours concernedly

Dr D Fox BSc, MD, CIEH

Dear President

It is with no regret and great relief that I submit my resignation as Captain and from the Committee. This is for personal and mental health reasons. May I wish my successor the wisdom of Solomon and the patience of Job.

Yours very sincerely

John Adams (Captain Ret'd)

HOLE 6

'Rabbits'

Par 3 Stroke Index 13

A Round with Alice

Do you remember when Michelle Wie and Annika Sorenstram had aspirations to challenge the men of the PGA Tour? I'm afraid this news came as a grave shock to Old Harry, Captain of our Seniors, when it was gleefully reported to him by the Lady Captain. Now, you must understand that Harry is not a misogynist – far from it. He trips the light fantastic with as many ladies as possible at the club's annual dinner dance, and is a thoroughly modern man who can even operate a smart phone but not, of course, within ten miles of the clubhouse.

On the other hand Harry is of the school which believes that golf and women don't mix. You can't get him to say why exactly but he will never tee off behind a ladies' four-ball, sniffs angrily if he hears a female voice when he is putting, and firmly believes that women shouldn't be tolerated on the course at weekends which is the only time a working man can play. You should appreciate that Harry retired from a successful career in banking 23 years ago. Of course, Harry's views cannot be justified today, can they? But, as one famous Asian professional golfer has proven since, he is not alone. For some reason, and I don't know what it is, lady golfers often carry a fearsome reputation.

Old Harry usually parks his Saab near the Artisans' hut, and the other day he overheard their Captain briefing his team before their annual match against the Ladies. 'This fixture,' he said, 'is one we have had for many years, and one we value highly and don't want to lose. So, for the benefit of those who haven't played in it before, watch the language. If I were you I would put cotton wool in my ears!'

There is also a story circulating in the Club that a younger lady, well, about forty-five actually, and a hopeful aspirant for membership, blighted her chances somewhat by taking a shower after a round. 'Who was that?' questioned one of the more mature lady members after this slip of a girl had left the changing room. 'I don't know,' replied her colleague, 'but I believe she wants to join.'

'Hmmm,' grunted the first, 'I'm not sure we want members who wear underclothes like that.'

On hearing about this, Old Harry opened a book on who this particular glamour girl could be, and what brand of double gusseted underwear would guarantee membership. His opinion was that any item bought on prescription from Boots would be appropriate.

Personally I have no objection to lady golfers. Indeed my best competition result was achieved in a mixed foursome – joint 18th if I remember correctly. My partner was an extremely keen player whose swing was somewhat limited by small hands and a large bust. A great theorist, she was convinced that the Harry Vardon overlapping grip would remedy the first problem but, unfortunately, the second prevented her checking it at the address. She overcame this, partly, by taking up her grip with the club held vertically above her head and then lowering it over and around her ample bosom.

Of course the whole sequence was not completed in one smooth movement, but rather in a series of wiggles and shrugs – and often repeated. For uphill lies and other situations where the position of the ball in relation to the feet is particularly significant, my assistance and advice was often invoked. The point of all this will become clear when you understand what happened at the short 14th. I mis-hit my tee shot into a bush which was separated from the green by a pond. I knew the best my partner could do was to hit the ball further into the bush or, worse, into the water.

'Alice,' I suggested tentatively, 'play an air shot. I can get it on the green.' She protested of course but in the end agreed, albeit reluctantly. Then she went through her preparations: up, grip, wiggle, slide etc. After the third run through my patience, understandably, wore thin. 'For goodness sake, Alice,' I whispered through clenched teeth, 'what is the problem?' 'Well,' she said, stepping back yet again, 'I'm really undecided on what club to use!'

On a final tack, I've just been skimming through the 1974 edition of the US *Golfers' Digest* (as one is wont to do) and was interested in an item on eighteen year old Laura Baugh ('rhymes with paw,' remember her?)

entitled *Not just another pretty face*. I learned that in her first six events on the LPGA Tour she banked over $9,000, combined beauty and brains by maintaining a near straight A average through high school and 'possessed the sexy golden blonde appeal her Long Beach upbringing suggests'. Further, 'Her provoking proportions and dimpled doll looks' had earned her *Golf Digest*'s Most Beautiful Golfer Award.

Even though a lady wrote this, I'm sure Old Harry, himself, would be happy that this attitude to sportswomen is unacceptable in the 21st century. Indeed, I believe he secretly hoped that Michelle would, eventually, get a top ten finish in a PGA event? 'Isn't that so, Harry? Harry, Harry where are you ...?'

HOLE 7

'Hot Stuff'

Par 4 Stroke Index 3

Golf was First Played in Scotland, Nonsense, Viva Mexico

The conquest of the Aztec empire by Cortez and his Conquistadors in the early 16th Century is one of the most tragic episodes of modern history. If that quest for gold and souls had not taken place we could now enjoy the full glory of the Mayan civilisation instead of the few tantalising ruined cities that remain, like Tikal in Guatemala, and Tulam and Uxmal in Northern Yucatan.

I first became interested in the expedition of Cortez who sailed from Cuba to Mexico in 1519, when completing my Spanish degree in Seville in the early 1960s. The major record of the chilling events was written by Cortez himself in a series of letters to Charles V but, as he was trying to ingratiate himself into the King's favour, it is suspected that the contents of the Cartas de Relación contained much fiction and many distorted facts. Still, they were interesting, and they helped with my thesis and the resulting reasonable degree which I managed to salvage from four years of drinking and poodle-faking at universities in England and Spain.

About eighteen months ago, while doing some more detailed background reading in preparation for a trip to Mexico that I had promised myself for many years, I came across a reference to a priest called Jeronimo de Aguilar who had interpreted for Cortez on his march from Yucutan to Tenochtitlan or Mexico City as it is now called. Jeronimo is a fascinating figure in his own right. Born in Ecija in Spain, and educated for the Church as a Franciscan friar, he was shipwrecked off the Yucatan coast in 1489. There were just fifteen survivors of the tragedy and of those who managed to reach the shore several subsequently died of exposure and others were eaten by cannibals. Fortunately, Jeronimo and his companion Gonzalo Guerrero, managed to escape inland where they were sheltered by Indians and gradually became assimilated into the Mayan culture. In truth, Gonzalo became more assimilated as he took a wife, or wives to be precise, whereas Jeronimo stuck to his religious vows and, much to the amusement of the native chief Xamanzana, remained celibate.

Life changed for him in a big way when, in 1519, he heard of Cortez landing on the Yucatan peninsula. While Gonzalo remained loyal to his Indian hosts and ultimately died fighting for them, Jeronimo journeyed to the coast to join Cortez, eventually finding him sheltering from a storm on the island of Cozumel, which the remarkable Jeronimo reached following a perilous journey in a canoe. Of course, Cortez welcomed him for his understanding of native culture and the priceless virtue of speaking several Indian languages; and so Jeronimo joined the expedition and marched with Cortez to Technochtitlan and became witness to the tragic events that unfolded.

Jeronimo's letters were written to another man of the cloth called Bartoleme de Olmedo, a priest who was the Chaplain to the expedition and a man much revered in the history of Spain because of his brave lone stand against some of the acts of oppression and cruelty that were perpetuated by Cortez. After the death of the Aztec Emperor, Montezuma, Bartoleme returned to Spain, eventually to Seville, while Jeronimo remained in Mexico to make a new life for himself. Strangely, he renounced his vows and married an Indian woman called Elvera Toznenetzin, raised a family and, thankfully, struck up an occasional correspondence with Bartoleme. It was in a copy of one of these letters, the originals of which are held in the Jesuit library in Seville, that I came across the following extract written about events in 1519:

> Some two days' march from Cholula, I was tasked to make my way from our encampment to a small village called Taxmula. There I was to ascertain the feelings of the Indians and barter for any provisions that they could supply, especially fruit. With a small escort of soldiers I left at dawn on the five league journey [about fifteen miles]. It was an arduous walk but in the late afternoon we began to see signs of cultivation and, eventually, Indians: a group of about twelve women. They appeared to be returning home from working in the fields but in doing so were making light of the journey through the distraction of a game of

skill. Of course, they were curious about us, but not frightened, and after a pause continued with their preoccupation.

It was some form of ball game at which they competed in teams of three or four. Each ball was about the size of a man's fist, bound in raffia, and marked with distinctive signs and colours. I watched as one woman placed her ball on one of the knee-high stone obelisks which marked the boundaries of each family's cultivated strip of land and then, using a short, hooked implement attached to her wrist with a cord, she swung two-handed at the ball inducing it to fly some 100 varas [a vara measures just under a metre] down the homeward track. One other from each team did the same with varying degrees of success but each strike was accompanied by shouts of exultation and glee or, if it was a poor one, by disparaging remarks and jeers.

The women then followed the balls until another member of the group struck the ball from wherever it lay. This sequence continued until the next obelisk was sighted, whereupon the next woman ready to play attempted to strike the ball, not for distance, but for accuracy in order to smite the marker. In God's name, Bartolome, I swear they demonstrated great skill, hitting it from a distance of five or six varas. I also observed that an older woman smoking a pipe was recording the strikes of each grouping by notching a stick. The action then proceeded again from the obelisk and, I assumed, continued until the women arrived home.

I have to say that I tried my hand at the game but with little success, missing the ball entirely twice and, much to the amusement of the women, smiting the obelisk firmly at the third attempt. However, it came to my attention that the effort of the game had caused the players to perspire freely and, as they were young and lightly clothed, I observed that the soldiers were becoming somewhat agitated. Partly for this reason, but mainly to complete my mission, I decided that it was time for us to move on. Nonetheless, Bartolome, I thought it best to record this interesting custom of the Cholula tribe having seen nothing like it in all my experiences in this land.

My holiday last year in Mexico, and in Peru where I climbed the trail to see Machu Picchu in all its glory, was wonderful. Throughout it, I had not thought about Jeronimo's 'game' at all, that is until I saw an exhibit in the National Museum of Anthropology in Mexico City. There in a cabinet was an object that matched exactly his description of the implement the Cholula women had used to hit the ball. It was described as 'A form of shepherd's crook designed to hold a ram by its horns'. It even had the hole where a cord or thong would have been looped. Later, just outside Cholula on the tiny site of what remains of the original Aztec settlement, I found among a pile of masonry a knee-high obelisk, very worn and marked with some incisions. The top was concave.

I took photographs of both these objects and when I returned home sent them to Padraigh O'Connell, Keeper of Mayan Antiquities at the British Museum. He explained that the 'crook' was a common tool of the Aztec period and, being fairly short was used to hold a ram still while it was stimulated to produce semen for artificial insemination purposes, a skill which contributed to the excellence of Mayan livestock. The obelisk was again a common object, used as Jeronimo had explained, to mark the ownership of cultivated strips. The part I had photographed was the inner core sunk into the ground, over which a wooden casing, coloured and marked to show the current owner, would have been placed. The details of both these items can be found in the *Dicciionario Porrua* should further reading be of interest.

As a keen golfer, my original reading of Jeronimo de Aguilar's account of the game had interested me greatly but the discovery of the obelisk and the shepherd's crook while travelling in Mexico was astounding. It seems very clear to me that a form of golf was well established in an ancient civilisation well before there was real evidence of such a game in Scotland and a full century before Paul Bril recorded a form of golf near Rome in his 1624 painting *Jeu de Mail*. It would also be natural for women, who were often involved in the husbandry of sheep, to adapt the tools of their trade for recreational purposes. Whatever, the game the Cholula women were playing had quite sophisticated rules which were a basis of competition as well as enjoyment. Further research may be necessary but there appears to be a very strong case for the Royal and Ancient to acknowledge this evidence and, at the very least, move its headquarters to Mexico!

HOLE 8

'Holly Bush'

Par 3 Stroke Index 17
Great Gifts for Gullible Golfers

With Christmas and birthdays in mind and the keen golfer always eager for any gadget to improve his game, why not take advantage of our new mail order catalogue designed for the ever hopeful hacker. Some real bargains are to be had and it is always good to be the first with a new toy. All prices include VAT and p&p except where stated otherwise.

Stocks are limited so rush your order in today quoting the order number.

Muttoff.
Nothing is a greater distraction to a round of golf than a badly behaved dog, one that is usually tethered to the bag of its equally badly behaved owner. Muttoff will emit a special high frequency sound which is only discernible to a dog and causes it to look seriously distressed. The owner will usually decide to take the animal home immediately. The operating instructions contain plausible veterinary advice that adds to the owner's concern and which you can use if he dithers. Our technicians are working on a similar device which will affect owners as well. £12.35 including presentation box. Probably no lasting effects. Made in Korea. D4543

RuleRef.
Attach this miniature camera and sound recorder to your cap and switch it on covertly whenever you foresee a possible breach of the Rules of Golf. RuleRef will record clearly the incident and prove that you were right when pointing out the violation to your partner or opponent. It is

41

also ideal for providing evidence of etiquette infringement. £65.75. Comes with leather case and free first aid kit. D6511

Periscope Range Finder.
This superbly engineered range finder is easily fitted to most trolleys. Extending electrically to a maximum height of three metres it is ideal for those infuriating blind holes and undulating courses. Submarine style handles either side of the view finder flick up and down at a touch, and focus and magnification are controlled by twist grip action. The graduated lens image guarantees accuracy of 3mm at 500 metres. A free, battered, U-Boat *Kapitän*'s cap with each purchase (while stocks last). £327.50. D1201

Puttaid.
Guaranteed to save at least five strokes a round this clever practice device combines a head torch and two spirit levels. Attach the spirit levels above each knee and focus the torch to shine on the ball. Hours of practice will ensure that your head and body remain perfectly still throughout the stroke. £21.00, batteries not included. Includes free booklet on the treatment of Sciatica. D8765

Natural Chameleon Skin Golf Glove.
A must for any discerning, fashion conscious lady golfer. This comfortable and rainproof glove changes colour to match whatever outfit you may be wearing, resulting in a tasteful, coordinated colourway. Fits all hand sizes. Buy two gloves and get one free. £15 each. 10% of the purchase price is donated to the Madagascan Wildlife Preservation Society. D1101

Pedashoes.
These stylish, waterproof golf shoes are both practical and fun. Manufactured to the highest quality in Mongolian yak hide, they feature a pedometer built into the toecap of the left shoe. Viewed through a small screen you can find out how far you have walked during your game. A sure-fire fitness aid and an ideal conversation piece at the nineteenth hole. Simple instructions for set-up to your length of pace. All sizes up to 12 and in three colours, black, white and co-respondents' tan and white. £65 a pair. D2400

Comfitrews.

A life changing accessory for the male golfer of advancing years, these comfortable, plaid plus fours feature a detachable incontinence pad in the crotch. Swing away with confidence once again! Available in three tartans: MacLean, MacDonald and Black Watch. Additional pads in the same tartans can be ordered separately in packs of twelve. Returns not accepted. £49.50 a pair. D4431
Pad packs 95p. D4433

RainGo, the high tech spectacle cleaner.

Simply a must for the visually challenged golfer. No more misted or rain spotted glasses holding up play while they are cleaned. This innovative, battery powered device fits under the peak of most baseball style caps and, at the touch of a remote button, directs a powerful jet of cleaning fluid onto the lenses followed immediately by a jet of warm drying air. Operating skills can be mastered in a few minutes. Recommended by the National Association of Romanian Eye Surgeons. £18.50. Batteries and cleaning fluid not included. D1020

Little Atom Ball Finder.

End the curse of lost balls once and for all. This handy two piece gadget will ensure that you find and identify your ball with ease however bad the rough. Just mark your ball using the radioactive paint contained in the dispenser. The other end of the dispenser contains a Geiger counter which emits a clicking sound which increases in intensity as you near your ball. Simple and effective and a real time-saver. Not recommended to be carried in the pocket. £23.75 plus p&p extra. Free lead-lined golfing glove with each purchase. D7789

Laughfix.

We have all experienced that embarrassing silence following one of the club Captain's pathetic jokes at the annual dinner. Save your conscience and his feelings with Laughfix. Containing a selection of male and female recorded laughs ranging from the hysterical to the faintly condescending, this amazing device will laugh for you. A clever safety feature ensures that it cannot be set off prematurely. £28.95 p&p extra. D3333

Borestopper.

Fed up with those old chestnuts badly told by Old Tom in the bar every weekend? Borestopper recognises 5000 old stories and displays the dreary punch line on a small LCD within seconds. You can then interject the punch line and ruin the joke. Old Tom won't chance his arm more than twice. No bigger than a credit card this amazing gadget can be kept to hand for any occasion. £15.75. Unbeatable value. D1111

All our gifts come with a full seven day guarantee.
Buy with confidence from us.

A Christmas Carol

Bad weather and the consequent club ban on electric trolleys has forced me into the annual transfer of kit and clubs from my large summer bag to my thin winter one. It is surprising what one finds! Anyway, with Christmas approaching I have set my summer bag discoveries to music and what better carol than the *Twelve Days of Christmas*. This is what the last verse of that wonderful old carol now should be.

On the twelfth day of Christmas
My golf bag gave to me:
12 toffees sticking
11 markers marking
10 balls a-smiling
9 stubby pencils
8 foreign coins
7 tatty tissues
6 Mars Bar wrappings
5 broken tees
4 scoring cards
3 dud pens
2 tatty gloves
And a plaster for a sore knee.

May you all enjoy your golf every day of the year.

HOLE 9

'Endeavour'

Practice Makes Perfect

Go to a professional tournament and stand for a couple of hours on the practice range. An hour or so before the players' tee time you will see our heroes making their way down with their caddies, coaches and, depending how famous they are, a number of indeterminate hangers-on. There follow some cheery greetings with other Pros, a few warming up exercises and then the practising begins. Short irons first, working up to the woods and sometimes vice versa. There is nothing hurried about this, there is pause for thought between shots, more chatting, some minor adjustments suggested by the coach and then, after ninety minutes of long, accurate and easy shot making, it's off to the practice green for a final 20 minutes putting before the tee time and the chance to make a million. Of course there's a pile of new balls available for each player, the caddy is on hand to place the balls on a tee and clean clubs and there is a pleasant five hour round ahead of you before another hour's fine tuning afterwards.

For we club hackers it is not quite the same. Get your tokens for the ball dispenser, fill a bucket of range balls which, shall we say, are not great quality and it's out to the driving range to practise all and each of the faults in your swing which you should be trying to cut out, not repeat. For most of us higher handicappers practising should be avoided at all costs. Besides which, it is a totally tedious pursuit like watching paint dry when standing in a draught. Just take a look around the practice area to see what I mean.

On the left there is Harry Kennedy, of course. Does he ever not practise? Harry is well retired, plays off 24 but once, in his prime, got down to 18. He has a bad hip, an arthritic neck and a prostate problem which means he must repair to the urinal between buckets of balls and on a cold day more often than that. And what is he practising? Well who knows? From a distance he could be cutting cane or beating a carpet, hardly worth the effort of bending down and balancing the ball on the tee.

At the other end is young David aged nine and a bit. He is swinging effortlessly with a shoulder turn so full that he is swinging well over 360 degrees and the ball flies off his club with a staccato crack. Harry's miserable thuds are so sad in comparison. Unfortunately, school, girls, work, family and other interests will define David's swing more than practice and if he keeps up the game he will change places with Harry in about sixty years. Then, of course, his arthritis of the neck will be worse because of modern man's penchant for spending hours hunched over laptops and smartphones.

There are a couple of ladies out too. Ladies practise in pairs, not to encourage or criticise each other or in the pursuit of a better technique but, rather, in order to engage in conversation. This is not a criticism of the ladies but is the result of an ingrained hereditary trait stemming from the time the ladies of the village met to do their laundry on the river bank. You can easily identify this connection with the past by the way they stop, flex their shoulders and backs and, especially rub their hands together at irregular intervals during practice. It may be mid-July on the course but their genes are telling them that the river water is bloody cold.

Ah, watch out, here comes Bernard Dunleary, handicap 9. He is playing against Jimmy James in the second round of the Gillespie Cup in ten minutes and must, must, hit a few balls before going out. The short time that he will be there will serve no purpose except to satisfy his under-standing that it is essential to loosen up before a match but the only certainty of his activity is that he will be late on the tee. Nevertheless Bernard, as rapidly as a Gatling gun, fires off his bucket of balls. He scarcely notices the flight and direction of his missiles and has no practice plan. Then he's off, well-satisfied and absolutely certain to hook his first drive into the long grass 120 yards up the fairway.

The 19 year old Assistant Pro is there too, grabbing the opportunity to play a few handsome shots before returning to the shop to release the Club Pro to teach a lesson. Since transferring between being a good amateur to a professional, the assistant's game has steadily declined at an inverse proportion to his skill at persuading club members that they look great in the new Gorex windcheaters or that the fashionable basket weave shoes give excellent ventilation in hot weather while remaining waterproof in a monsoon.

But it is on the putting green that most damage is done. There are two tribes of practice putters. On the left of the green are the self-convincers who ring a hole with balls and spend hours holing out from two feet. On the right are the optimists who always practise the long 60 footers. But, beware, there is a physical penalty to pay for both activities. An hour crouched in that stiff-armed, hunchbacked, bent kneed, crablike pose which the amateur putter adopts will cause huge and irreparable skeletal and muscular damage and it won't improve their putting, which only matters six to ten feet from the hole anyway.

Once or twice a year the practice area comes into its own. That, of course, is when there is a club manufacturer's day. Advertised by the Pro well in advance, the manufacturer brings a lorry load of the new model clubs for the members to try. These range from drivers made out of materials nobody's ever heard of and with sweet spots that Mae West could only dream about, through irons with low centres of gravity and built in Zenith flex to prevent hooking or slicing, and putters that can double up as branding irons or instruments of torture. The gullible members flock in their dozens to slash and whirl these new weapons while the experts from the manufacturers call encouragement from the sidelines. They will even weigh you, take your inside leg measurement and calculate your kinetic torsion ratio in order to get just the club for you. And do they work? Of course; just take a look at Harry Kennedy up there on the left. He bought that new driver yesterday and it's added, well, absolutely nothing to his game.

But there again, there is nothing wrong with the club, he just can't get on with it!

HOLE 10

'Patience'

Par 4 Stroke Index 12

The Grudge Match

Vernon Kane looked at the draw on the competition notice board. He loved the annual Fairchild Medal but had not had the chance to play in it for a couple of years. In fact he didn't play singles very much at all these days but this one appealed to him. After all he had won it about nine years ago. He ran his finger down the starting sheet and saw his name drawn against ... oh no! This can't be right, not Colin Tanker. 'I can think of a more appropriate name for him,' he muttered. Of all the people who had entered, of all the people in the club, in the bloody world in fact, he was drawn to play with Colin bloody Tanker.

Now let's put this in perspective shall we? Vernon is a nice guy, a reasonable golfer, a father and husband and he has never been in serious trouble with the police, but if there is one person he can't stand playing with it's Colin Tanker. There is no logical reason for this, for in his way Colin is also a nice chap, loved by his wife (and mistress as well we suspect) and he plays a steady game. But to Vernon he is anathema, mark 1, with brass knobs on. Everything about him grates: his prissy little moustache, his stupid hat and, especially, his detailed understanding and interpretation of the rules. He was to be avoided at all costs and at all times. By this time Vernon is irrationally cross and ready to scratch and is feverishly searching for a pen when the Captain comes in with Colin.

'Ah, Vernon,' he beamed, 'I was just telling Colin here that we had a full list for the Fairchild and it should now be up. I was delighted when you told me last week that you were going to enter. Previous winners are always welcome.'

Vernon's false smile suggested more of a Transient Ischaemic Attack than an indication of pleasure and he clenched his buttocks as he had been advised to relieve stress and blood pressure on long-haul flights. He mumbled something or other and made a quick exit. Colin looked at the list and went white. 'Vernon Kane, of all people … Anyone but Vernon bloody Kane.' He shook his head and continued shaking it throughout his short drive home.

The day of the match dawned bright and warm, a perfect spring day for golf in fact, but this was not reflected in the faces or the body language of the gladiators as they trudged their way to the first tee. 'You're 17 aren't you, Vernon? And I'm 16 so you get one shot.' 'Why state the obvious,' thought Vernon. 'Our handicaps were on the starting list and on the cards.' He tried to calm himself as he waited for Colin to drive. What is more he tried to ignore the meticulous preparation which went into each and every single one of Colin's shots: the precise placing of the tee and the ball on it, the step back to point the club up the fairway to gauge the direction of flight, the three careful practice swings, the ludicrous shifting of the buttocks to settle the stance and the exasperating long, posed wait after the stroke until the ball comes to rest; totally and eternally to rest.

'We'll be here all day now, thought Vernon as he trudged up the first and the second hole was no better. Colin was one of those chaps who had head covers on all his clubs. So, after consulting the card to check the stroke index, absolutely necessary as he had only been a member for twenty years, he went through the usual 'tee ceremony' as meticulously as a geisha girl in Kyoto entertaining the head of Myango Motors. But, before striking the ball, he stepped back and changed his club, carefully replacing the cover on the discarded one and slotting it in the bag. Vernon sighed in exasperation.

They both were bunkered and Vernon was told in no uncertain terms that he was in danger of 'building a stance' as he prepared to play his ball which was in the face of the bunker. He said nothing however when Colin carefully repaired a stud mark on his line of putt on the pretence that it was a pitch mark. 'It's damn good that the greens are not tined otherwise he would repair all those as well,' thought Vernon.

And so the game progressed, painfully. Twice Colin told Vernon to move because he could see him on his backswing, and twice Vernon glowered when a ripped zip fastener opened another compartment in

Colin's capacious bag. A more serious argument arose on the 7th when Vernon was accused of unfairly taking his stance. It happened like this.

Vernon's drive, slightly hooked, fell at the base of a young tree whose foliage was developing strongly in the spring sunshine. With a short iron in his hand he took up his stance backing into the tree and ensuring that on his backswing he would not strike any branch or dislodge any blossom. It was still a tricky shot but he felt confident in trying it. His opponent, however, was not happy and protested that he had not fairly taken up his stance according to Rule 13. 'Yes, I have moved the branches with my back as I took up my stance but I have to in order to "fairly" take it up.' 'But you are not allowed to bend, move or break anything fixed or growing' insisted Colin, 'and you are.'

'I haven't broken anything or defoliated a single stem. I'm only taking up my stance as I'm entitled,' fumed Vernon. 'Well, you should be penalised two strokes,' said Colin, 'and that is what I will record.' And he stormed off. Tight-lipped, Vernon recorded the score as a six and not an eight.

On the next hole, after Colin had driven, Vernon said, 'and that's a two stroke penalty for you as well.' Colin looked at him, 'What for?'

'Well, when taking up your stance you bent a daisy under your foot on the tee.'

'But I was just taking up a fair stance and you have to stand on the grass.'

'Moving bending or breaking anything growing is improving the stance so it's a two shot penalty for you.'

'But that's ridiculous as each of us from now will be penalised when we bend the grass. We couldn't play at all if that was the case.'

'Right,' fumed Vernon, 'that's the whole point about fairly taking up your stance which is what I was doing against that tree. We'll settle this with the Pro afterwards.'

And so, dear reader, the game progressed but hardly in accordance with the spirit of the game as visualised by the R&A. There was rapidly diminishing courtesy and little sportsmanship. Certainly discipline, especially self-discipline, proved to be wanting. Tempers and swings shortened as they hacked and cleaved their miserable way up the fairways and the volume and frequency of expletives increased. What should have been a 'Nip and Tuck' affair rapidly turned into an 'S**t and F**k' one.

And then came the incident of the 'Hole made by a burrowing animal.' It was on the 17th when Vernon's drive finished in such an obstruction. 'I get relief from this,' he informed his glowering opponent.

'What for?'

'I can't play this, it's in a hole.'

'But that's not a hole made by a burrowing animal.'

'Colin, what makes you so bloody sure of that?'

'There are no droppings.'

'That's not the rule. It's for a burrowing animal; shit's got nothing to do with it.'

'Yes, but that would prove it, wouldn't it? We'd see rabbit droppings.'

'Not if it was a mole or a groundhog, or a gopher or salamander or if the bloody animal did its muck down the hole. It might have been in bed when it was taken short. It lives down there, sometimes for hibernation it lives down there for bloody weeks or months. It's not going to come up for a crap in the middle of the night just in case it has to prove to an arsehole like you that this is where it lives.'

'It could have been a dog or a cat and that is not a burrowing animal.'

'Well, where's the dog or cat shit then? It's a hole, a scrape and any reasonable person would accept it. But not you, bloody Colin bloody Tanker with your stupid hat and prissy little moustache and ...'

And then Vernon stopped and grabbed at his chest. He groaned, a sheen of sweat on his brow and he fell to the ground breathing rapidly. 'My God, a heart attack,' thought Colin and he dropped to one knee and grabbed Vernon's hand. 'Vernon can you hear me? Can you lift your arms, stupid question but can you smile?'

Vernon didn't answer but continued to groan and was obviously in great pain. Colin looked around but there was no one near so he reached to his bag, loudly unzipped a pocket and pulled out his mobile and dialled 999.

'Ambulance, yes. My friend is having a heart attack or stroke, come now it is really urgent ... No, we are on the golf course, the 17th fairway.' He looked around. 'Yes ... that's right, it runs alongside Meadow Road and there is a gate onto the course near the bus stop. Yes. I'll stay on the phone but hurry.'

He turned back to Vernon, checked his breathing and then pulled him into a sitting position against his trolley. He remembered this from his first aid days at work. 'Hurry up with the ambulance,' he called into his phone, 'he is looking awful, grey and his breathing is very faint.'

'Stay with it, Vernon, the ambulance is on its way, you'll be OK.' And then he saw that Vernon had stopped breathing. 'He's not breathing,' he shouted into the phone and he pulled Vernon towards him, lifted his neck and breathed deeply into his mouth checking to see that his chest was rising. He did this three or four times and then tried some pushing on his chest. Then back to the breathing. Just then three things happened. Vernon coughed, gasped for breath and, to his relief, Colin heard the sound of the ambulance approaching. Soon the medics were there and he sat back shaking with relief and effort. Some other players had assembled by now and they helped Colin to his feet trying to reassure him. They watched in silence as Vernon was wheeled off under the care of the ambulance men.

Four days later Vernon was sitting up in bed in the Cardiac wing of the local hospital when Colin came in. They looked at each other and Colin sat down on the chair beside the bed. 'How are you feeling?'

'OK Colin, and thanks, I owe my life to you.'

Colin nodded and helped himself to a grape. 'I've been thinking you know, Vernon. Regardless of whether or not that was a hole made by a burrowing animal, I was one up with one to go when you left the course without specific permission from the committee. And you haven't reported to them since. I believe that constitutes conceding the game.'

Vernon looked at him. Was that a smile on his face when he said that? Surely a heart attack constitutes a good reason and ...

'Yes Colin, I think you're right under Rule 6-8.' He put out a weary hand. 'Congratulations.'

Colin helped himself to another grape and then he really smiled.

HOLE 11

'Relaxez-Vous'

New Regulations for Slow Play

Slow play is a major concern to players and officials. The five to six hour round is not unusual in professional competitions and many clubs are experiencing tedious, extended rounds in club competitions and the Sunday four-ball. The R&A has long been concerned with this unwelcome trend and in Section 1 of the Rules of Golf, Etiquette: Behaviour on the Course, their advice on Pace of Play is clear. Unfortunately, it is often ignored. The R&A have accepted that if they cannot persuade golfers to avoid slow play then they may have to regulate them. The new rules, if adopted, will be used in both professional and amateur slow play competitions.

Rules of Golf Appendix IV; Accepted Rules of Slow Play

Definitions
All defined terms are in *italics* and are listed alphabetically in the Definitions Section.

Rule 1. The Teeing Ground
   a. No slow player will approach the *teeing ground* until it is completely clear of other players. The initial approach will be made without a club or ball in order for the player to ascertain the direction and distance of the next hole. The player may then return to his bag to select the required club and a ball.
   b. After teeing-up the slow player must retreat at least ten metres keeping the ball and the intended target in line and consider the shot for

an appropriate length of time. He may then select another club or put on his glove, or both, before *addressing the ball* for the first time. A player may step back from the *address* no more than three times.

c. A player may have no more than six practice swings and five *jiggles* before the final address which must last at least twenty seconds before the *stroke* is made. The player must retain his position on the *teeing ground* until ten seconds after the ball has come to rest.

d. On returning to his bag, the player will return the club to the correct slot in no more than three attempts. All clubs, including irons, will have head covers which require careful replacement. Before moving to his ball the player will remove his glove, adjust his clothing and consult his score card.

PENALTY FOR BREACH OF RULE

For the slow player – none.

For following players – a hint of impending doom.

Rule 2. The Walk

a. A measured pace is to be maintained but never directly to where the ball has come to rest. Should a *partner* be required to play first, the slow player must never walk forward of him regardless of whether or not his ball is in line of play.

b. Within ten metres of his ball the slow player will reduce his pace appreciably before circling his ball in order to examine the ground around it. Before playing the ball, procedures prior to the *address* as set out in Rule 1 of this Annexe will be adopted.

c. At no time during the walk will the player consider which club to use next, or acknowledge the presence of anyone else playing with or behind him.

PENALTY FOR BREACH OF RULES

For the slow player – none.

For following players – at least two shots dropped through rising exasperation.

Rule 3. Searching for Lost Balls

a. In searching for a *lost ball* the slow player will conform to Rule 12. In addition he must:

(1) Never take his bag to within fifty metres of the search area.

(2) Never carry a suitable iron or two that may be used when the ball is found.

(3) Always search assiduously for a ball in Stableford Competitions when he is already three over par for that hole.

PENALTY FOR BREACH OF RULE

For the slow player – none.

For following players (now two groups of four-balls) – some shared blaspheming and an increase in the floridity of the complexion of any retired Major.

Rule 4. The Putting Green

a. Approach.

When approaching the *putting green* the slow player will ascertain the route to the next hole and position his bag/trolley on the opposite side of the *green* to it. He will then approach his ball on a circuitous route from beyond the flag at times stooping, or moving backwards or sideways to establish the contours of the green from all angles, except that of his *line of putt*, taking care to remove all *loose impediments* anywhere on the green.

b. Preparation.

(1) On reaching his ball he will mark it carefully and take it to his bag to clean. The cleaning process will not start until it is his turn to putt. After cleaning, he will replace his ball so that the maker's name, or any self-inscribed mark is lined up exactly on the calculated putting line. This may be adjusted no more than four times. The player will then enter the final phase of lining up. This must include:

(a) Calculating the line from the other side of the pin, from both sides and again from behind the ball.

(b) Kneeling or crouching using the putter as a plumb-line or as a prop preferably on someone else's line.

(c) Removing the pin to gaze into the hole.

(d) Marking his ball carefully before adjusting its line following the second deliberation.

(e) Retreating to the edge of the green to ask his partners if it is his turn.

c. The putt and sequential actions.

(1) Unless a putt is *holed*, the slow player must not follow the ball immediately. Instead he may check the line and practise his stroke a minimum of three times before marking his ball and lining up again until such time as the putt is holed. In match play it is essential to hole out even though the putt is given.

(2) Before leaving the green two more practice putts are permitted to ensure the line is noted for future play. The score should be registered before moving to the player's bag/trolley and the score card checked while ambling along the front of the *green* to the next hole.

PENALTY FOR BREACH OF RULE

For the slow player – none.

For the following groups (now 3) – Much angry discussion and the suggestion of an apoplectic seizure by the Major.

Rule 5. Equipment

a. The Glove.

The glove must never be put on until immediately before the *address* and removed prior to the walk. It must be removed one finger at a time prior to putting and placed partly in the hip pocket.

b. Tees and Markers. These must always be difficult to get at, often necessitating the removal of the glove or a search in the bag. When waterproof trousers are adopted during a round, *tees and markers* must be left in the pocket of the normal trouser in order to make them even more difficult to get at.

c. Spectacles.

Spectacles must always be cleaned, whatever the weather conditions, after the first *address* and before the *stroke*. In wet weather the club may be leaned against the player's thigh while the cleaning process is conducted so that it invariably falls to the ground necessitating the use of a towel to dry the grip.

d. Measuring devices (MD).

MDs should be used prior to every shot and the distance passed to anyone within earshot. It is especially important to measure the distance from tee to pin on par fives. If the ball falls appreciably short or overshoots the green, the distance should be checked again.

e. The scorecard. For accuracy it is preferable to mark the score card on the *green* or close to it. This will render unlikely a false score being recorded due to a lapse of memory. The running total will be checked at least four times per round prior to the address. At the conclusion of the round the score card will be completed on or close to the *green*.

PENALTY FOR BREACH OF RULES

For the slow player – none.

For the following groups (now four) – two broken clubs, a damaged tree, a bruised dog and a limping Major.

Rule 6. Awareness

Except in the unlikely event that he might drive-through or hit a player in a preceding group, the slow player is to be totally unaware of other players including his *partners*. The only exception to this rule will be in the bar after the game when he will ask the Major (retired) if he's had an enjoyable morning.

HOLE 12

Good Health

Par 4 Stroke Index 4

A Conversation with a Master of Wine

When I was a young man, and that was quite some time ago, I never mentioned that I was a keen golfer to any of the girls whom I dated. You see, unlike today, golf wasn't synonymous with glamour and money and its players weren't celebrities. Rugby, soccer, even cricket were sports that would impress a lady but golf, with its image of old men, pipes and baggy trousers, no way. After all, I am sure no modern stud would try and pull a 'chick' in clubland (and I don't mean the golf course) by explaining that he was not into 'throwing a few shapes tonight, luv, as I have an important lawn bowls match tomorrow.'

In those times entertaining was different as well. For example, when you took a girl out to dinner you paid, she didn't. It was only after a few dates that young Sheila might suggest going halves, which of course you refused. In some restaurants there were even two menus, one with the prices on, and one without; and guess who was handed the priced one by the snooty waiter? An early skill I developed was to remain expressionless as I cast my eye down the expensive list, and refrain from wincing when Sheila innocently ordered a costly one.

Ordering the wine was always a stressful moment, worse than lining up that fourth vital putt. For some reason you imagined everyone would sense your ignorance but as chances happen, the waiter, let alone your girl friend, probably knew as little as you. I well remember ordering a dessert wine with a main course, a curry, and compounding the embarrassment by spooning the second highly flavoured course onto Sheila's plate, only to find that it was the hot towels we were supposed to use to wipe our face and hands.

And that brings me to the point of this article. Wine is still surrounded by mystery and mystique that can be a bit off-putting, but it is also a familiar part of most of our lives. Knowing a little more about it might not matter in the conquest of the modern breed of golf babe but it will certainly ensure greater enjoyment and, probably, better value when drinking the stuff. I was delighted, therefore, to be able to put a few questions to a Master of Wine over lunch at one of Hertfordshire's fine courses.

David Vintner (and that is what I will call him) started off his working life as an accountant but soon decided that 'bean counting' was out, but the grape was in. 'I drank wine occasionally at home,' he said, 'became more interested in it through friends at college, but it was a really knowledgeable buyer for a major wine importer who instilled in me a passion for wine which I have retained ever since.'

A passion, it must be said, that over a quarter of a century has seen him rise through the industry to become, among other achievements, an Executive Director of the Institute of Masters of Wine. 'Their qualifying examination,' said David, 'is the toughest professional exam I have ever sat.'

'If I could afford it, I would really like to buy fine wines,' I said, downing yet another glass of the club's excellent house red, 'but I usually buy wine in the £6 to £8 range from the local supermarket. Do I get good value for money?'

'Well,' said David, 'Duty and the VAT on the Duty is about £2.50, packaging and shipping costs probably account for another £1.25 and the margins for the producer, importer and retailer a further £1.25, so you see the cheaper the bottle the poorer the wine you have for the cost. I would say that the more you pay up to about £12.00 a bottle, the better the value. After that, the selling price is not always linked to cost. In a restaurant paying more to get better wine value holds good up to about £35.00.'

'So what about the £200 bottle we hear about; is that really worth it?'

'If you can afford it for the special occasion, the answer is probably yes. But it's a risk because the retailer won't take it back if you don't like it. If you want to go down that line, buy from an established independent merchant who knows the bottle's history and who has controlled it properly from original shipment. It's a bit like buying a car from a reputable dealer.'

'But for the man in the street the supermarket is a good place to buy, right?' I said.

'Absolutely; I believe that the supermarkets set fair margins for the everyday drinker. Waitrose and Tesco have the widest range, and a panel of their own Masters of Wine approves all their products. I would also say that their monthly promotional offers are the result of good deals that they have struck with producers and are good value for the consumer. For fine wines for that special occasion however, I repeat, use an established independent dealer.'

'A lot of talk about wine revolves around the label. Is it wrong, then, to use a decanter.'

'There are only two rationales for decanting wine; first to get rid of the sediment in an old red wine or a port and, second, if contact with air will enhance the wine. This usually only applies to expensive, young wines. In all other circumstances use the bottle. Incidentally (and here DV looked at me quizzically), on the odd occasion when you don't intend to finish the bottle at one sitting, pour the balance into a clean half bottle for storage overnight. It will prevent oxidation and stay fresh for up to two days in the fridge.'

'I'll bear that in mind, David,' thinking 'when did I ever leave a half bottle?' Then quickly moving on, 'how do you tell if a wine is corked or, perhaps, is just a rotten product?'

'That is a very good question and a tricky one to answer. Corked means that the chemical treatment to neutralise the cork as a raw material has left traces of the process in the cork which, in turn, interacts with the wine and makes it taste as it shouldn't. Smelling the cork or the bottle is useless, and so is smelling the wine immediately the bottle is opened. After fifteen minutes or so the smell will come through but you can only really tell by the taste. I repeat, it should taste like you expect it to. Remember, screw caps can't give a corked wine and are no longer prejudicial to quality.'

'Can we at home get the best out of our bottle by serving it at the right temperature, and if so, what should that be?'

David thought as he sipped his glass. 'Red wines should be served at room temperature,' he said, 'but remember, that's room temperature before central heating became the norm. There is a tendency for red wines to be served too warm and white ones too cold, you know direct from the fridge. As a general rule both reds and whites should be served at the same temperature they're at when removed from the cellar or cool storage room. Also, always store wines on their side. Port, sherry, spirits and so on should be stored upright.'

'Ah, that reminds me, perhaps we should have something to go with our coffee, an Armagnac perhaps? We're not driving after all. And while we are waiting perhaps you can tell me about champagne, surely it's just the name that attracts the price, isn't it?'

'The champagne method is the best way to make champagne, and the Champagne region makes the best Champagnes. Having said that, you can get some very good champagne method outside the region. Sparkling wines are of lower quality wherever they come from.'

'I quite like Prosecco,' I thought, but went on to say, 'When I was a lad, ordering wine in a restaurant with aloof waiters could be an ordeal. Luckily, Mateus Rosé appeared on the scene. Not only was it cheap, but the bottle provided the major source of table lamps in every girl's flat I visited. What about today, should we settle for the restaurant house wine or is it a sticking line they want to move, and what about the waiter's recommendation?'

'It depends how serious the restaurant is about its wine. House wines should be quaffable and have no distinctive characteristics. After all everyone has to like them so that the restaurant can sell a lot, and although normally the cheapest, they are not the best value. A waiter's recommendation is fine provided it's within your budget and he knows what he is talking about.'

'What about tasting and smelling it when it is served. Isn't that a bit pretentious?'

'Pretentious, *moi*! If it is a reasonable wine why not? But make sure, though, that the waiter puts enough in the glass for a proper sample: smell it to see if it is attractive, taste it to see if it is at the right temperature and tastes acceptable to you, and move it around a bit to bring in the air. But you know, the best place to enjoy and taste a good wine is at home.'

'OK, so when I'm at home pouring wine for my friends, how much should I put in the glass?'

'I could talk for hours about the pros and cons of glasses and their shapes but at home generosity, or the lack of it, comes into play, while in the restaurant it's all about cost and value. As a rule of thumb, fill a glass about half full. Restaurants will fill the glass, but it will be a small one and, of course, the waiter will keep refilling it!'

'What about buying wines by the glass in a restaurant. Is that safe or will I be getting someone else's dregs?'

David nodded. 'Sometimes it is prudent to order a glass before you order a bottle, especially where house wine is concerned. You can always ask when the bottle was opened, particularly so when you are having an early lunch or dinner when the restaurant may have opened some bottles well in advance or even the night before. The real safeguard is to ask for the bottle to be opened at your table. You should always expect that when ordering a whole bottle.'

'The Sunday papers are always full of recommendations, vintages, what to lay down for the future and so on. How should mortal wine man take these suggestions?'

'You get some good tips from these articles, but remember the writers are paid to write wines up. Buy one to start with and if you like it, buy more, and if you really like it buy a good supply because others will have read the same article and stocks won't last. Don't even think of laying down a wine under £12.00 and as far as vintage is concerned it matters for European wines, but not so much for New World wines where climatic conditions are more stable.'

'So would you recommend New World wines?'

'Of course. As I have said the climate is more regular, in many cases the methods used are more modern than in the Old World and there is no legislative structure such as Appellation Contrôlée. The market decides what is good. In my view some of the best wines around at this time are from Chile priced between £6.00 and £8.00.'

'Now I know, David, that a few years ago you trained as a professional chef at Leith's School of Food and Wine. Why did you do this when at the top of a career in wine? Have you any tips about the right wines with the right food?'

'To answer your first question, I felt that after a lifetime in the trade I knew 95 per cent about wine but only about five per cent about food and, as you know, the two go together. There's an awful lot of emotional clutter surrounding both topics so, in all seriousness I say eat and drink what you like. Conventions are there to be broken and, in any case, the sauces not the fish or the meat can often dictate the choice of wine. Why not try smoked salmon with sherry or port?'

'I will, but where do you want to go next in the wine business?'

'Literally, I want to get back to the roots of the trade and run my own vineyard in Burgundy. I want to get my hands dirty again.'

'Well, I wish you luck with that, David. Thanks for a great lunch and a most interesting conversation. Now, how about a Kümmel before we play nine holes this afternoon?'

Three Kümmels later it was getting too dark to play golf, thankfully. Sheila should be here to pick us up soon.

HOLE 13

'New Fields'

Par 5 Stroke Index 18
Travel Time

Fort Eustis, Virginia is a US Army training establishment in the southern state of Virginia. It is colloquially known by the 'inmates' by the more descriptive name of Fort Uterus, Vagina. By any standards it is huge, boasting a small airport, a heliport, a small dockyard and, in its prime in the 1970s when I was there, host to 40,000 students a year on a variety of military courses. It also boasted a very nice 18 hole golf course. The year 1976 saw the 200th anniversary of the American Revolutionary War and the birth of the nation. We Brits call it the War of Independence. Anyway, this anniversary seemed to take over the whole of the United States. Everywhere I looked I was reminded of it and the golf course was no exception. The flags on every hole were marked with the words '1776-1976, 200 years of the American Nation' but at that time, of course, the Americans were British and Cornwallis's British army consisted mainly of Hanoverian and French mercenaries. In reality the Brits thrashed the Huns and the Frogs, as ever. Nevertheless, I felt personally responsible for the humiliation marked by this celebration. Indeed, I believe that the strain of putting against this constant reminder of a British defeat ruined my skills around the green forever.

Thankfully the Royal Navy came to my rescue. The Aircraft Carrier HMS *Ark Royal*, the pride of our fleet, and we had one at the time, sailed into Newport News naval base just down the road from us. Clearly painted on her sides in huge letters were the words '876-1976 eleven hundred years of the Royal Navy.'

But I digress. Golf in Virginia could be a sticky affair as in summer the temperatures and the humidity were very high and the despised buggy was an essential. So too was the pitcher of beer with a little salt in it to wash down our chilli burgers after a sweaty game. One day I drove up to the course which seemed strangely deserted but there was unusual activity in the car park. Players were leaving their cars and then making a mad dash into the clubhouse with their arms thrashing the air around them. I could not fathom why until I got out of my car. I was immediately covered in a swarm of small black flies, nasty biting flies it seemed, so I too made a dash for shelter and, like everyone else, arrived in the clubhouse covered in the little varmints.

Of course there was no chance of playing that day and that must have upset the Commanding General who was a very keen golfer indeed. How do I know? Well later that afternoon a C130 Hercules originally equipped to spray defoliant on the canopy jungles hiding the Viet Cong in that dreadful war made several low passes over the course spraying something or other that killed the plague of flies in their millions, birds and wildlife too probably and perhaps the odd soldier still braving the insects. The General's regular golfing partner also commanded the Air Force base at Langley which was located on the York Peninsula just down the road from us so his assistance was, no doubt, requested and enthusiastically given. Only in the USA!

The great Wentworth Club has been in the news recently for all the wrong reasons. Thankfully, all seems to be peace and reconciliation for now. The courses are wonderful and the clubhouse facilities second to none but I remember playing there many moons ago when the clubhouse was being refurbished and a great deal of it was displaced into Portakabins – dozens of them all linked together on a grand scale. Now, I've lived in many different sorts of huts during my service in the army, including Portakabins, but this was the first time that I had ever lost my way in one and been forced to ask for directions.

Muirfield is another great, traditional club with as many quirks and surprises in the clubhouse as there are on the wonderful and challenging course itself. Playing in the Army meeting some years back I was very surprised to find there was no bar in the Smoke Room but, instead, a structure was wheeled out to cater for brandies and liqueurs. There was no pro shop either so you had to drive to Gullane to buy a ball.

However, that is not the point of this story. This annual gathering of the Army Officers' Golfing Association brought together a mixture of young and old, senior and junior and some real old buffers wearing golf outfits more associated with Braid, Taylor and Vardon than a modern fighting force. One conversation in the changing room sticks in the memory.

'Don't I know you? Weren't you in the 17th Indian Division at some time?'

'Yes, I was, and who are you then?'

'Davidson, Charlie Davidson, 63rd Brigade, Gurkhas, and you're ...?'

'Andrews-Smythe, Mike.'

'So it is, so it is, good to see you again, Mike.'

'You must remember old Ben Hallam then, wasn't he a chum of yours?'

'Well, I knew him, not a chum really; strange fellow, hated elephants.'

Moving around as I did, it was sometimes a bit tricky to get into a golf club. I had some hopes of success when, following a posting to Surrey, I happened to hear of a new course which was looking for members. It was fairly near my house so one evening I popped along to recce the situation. A rather grand entrance greeted me and it led me to a modern looking club house which I went into. It was soulless and, worse, the walls were decorated with a wallpaper featuring golfers in various outfits in the middle of swings of one sort or another. A bank of slot machines furnished one wall. There was one occupant. He was a tall, grey haired gentleman clad entirely in white: shirt, pullover, white plus twos, white socks and shoes and standing next to him was a great white Borzoi hound.

The hound was attached to a chain as was, I noticed, its owner but his was thick, gold and very ornate and worn around his neck. I knew instinctively that in the trolley park would be a white bag and each club, including irons, would have a monogrammed head cover. This was not for me, so I left. Sure enough, there was the white bag on an immaculate trolley accompanied by one or two similar chariots and their tawdry accoutrements.

In Colchester in the late 1960s I managed to join the prestigious Frinton Golf Club, a delightful course in a genteel town without a pub, I believe, and at that time with signs on the manicured grass verges saying 'Please do not walk on the green sward.' Certainly it was rumoured that seagulls had to invert when flying over the clubhouse. Most summer weekends I would motor to it in my battered Austin 1100 along the narrow roads from Colchester doing my best to avoid the burgeoning gridlock of the holiday traffic. A friend, who was in the Army Catering Corps and married to a glamorous Swedish lady who did gymnastics on the beach in a very skimpy bikini, knew that I was a keen golfer and asked if I would take a house guest of his along for a round at the weekend.

'No problem,' I said, 'I'll call round and pick him up at about 7:30 on Sunday morning.'

'Don't you bother,' he replied, 'you're on the way so he will use his car and collect you,' which he did, in a luxurious and very expensive Rolls Royce.

The journey to Frinton with my new chum, a Harley Street specialist it turned out, was a pleasure, with no traffic hold-ups as, I swear, the police gave us priority at all the junctions. So, unruffled and cool we rolled into the club's car park with plenty of time to spare. Now, in the year that I had been a member of the club I had always been directed by the attendant to the furthest end of the car park, under the lime trees along with the rest of the Austins and Morrises and other plebeian carriages of the not so rich, but not this time. With an obsequious flourish we were waved into a spot next to the Captain's reserved space, gliding into it just as he was emerging from his Humber. He waited until we alighted from our magnificent machine and introduced himself to my guest who, graciously, introduced him to me, and we shook hands, a pleasure that had eluded us both until that moment. We joined him for coffee as well.

I was never afforded that welcome again!

Golf in Germany was very much an upper-social strata game when I played there. We in the military got a special dispensation on the fees which made membership of the lovely nine hole Munster course possible. The car park was full of top class BMWs and Mercedes but there was also a good sprinkling of Ferraris, Porsches and a nice Jensen Interceptor. The clubhouse was very comfortable, chic possibly, and the members were pleasant and exceedingly welcoming to me. My 'Get me by German' was hardly needed as nearly everyone spoke excellent English. In a match against a very exclusive club in Bad Pyrmont I recall that I was given a small 'goodie bag' before setting out on my round. It included a couple of balls, some tees, a ball marker and a bottle of deodorant. I was about to take this personally until I found out that this was standard issue.

In 1967 Britain's military presence East of Suez was coming to an end. We seemed to be fighting against groups of initials as the slogans of those wishing our removal from that barren rock spent a lot of time and paint writing their propaganda on the walls of many buildings. 'FLOSY says get out you Imperialist dogs' and 'NLF Rules'. These slogans stood for 'The Federation for the Liberation of Southern Yemen' and the 'National Liberation Front.' There were other sub-sects with hostile intent who must all have been perplexed when a new sign appeared in various places, 'NAAFI forever'. The Navy, Army and Air Force Institute was of course the soldiers' canteen. Squaddie humour at its best.

The golf course was set in a patch of scrubby desert close to the RAF airfield at Khormaksar and it consisted of sand fairways and sand greens called 'browns' because they were sprayed with engine oil to give a very decent putting surface. Crystalline salt pockets made up the bunkers. All players carried a patch of imitation grass carpet to play from the fairways and all the 'browns' were manned by small boys who spent their day like oxen at a well, hauling lengths of hessian round and round so that there would be a smooth surface for the following players.

A couple of the holes ran alongside the airfield whose perimeter fence was protected by an anti-personnel minefield complete with the usual skull and crossbones warning signs.

Running parallel to these were yellow posts marking the Out of Bounds in golfing parlance. It was not unusual to see quite a few shiny white golf balls lying in the sand of the minefield at the end of a day's play but not even the most impecunious of us was prepared to chance retrieving one even if it were within a foot or so of the markers. Strangely enough there were usually none there the following morning but there were quite a few small boys selling 'pick ups' on the first tee.

I bought my first set of new golf clubs in Aden, in the famous Crescent where you could buy anything! It was a half-set of Japanese manufacture and it cost me £8 including the bag. I played my best round ever with those clubs.

Bay Point on the Gulf Coast of the USA was a very nice complex with lots of lakes, some of them sporting alligators I recall. I was somewhat mystified by a loud, thunderous drumming noise which occurred at regular intervals during my round. Then all became clear as a golf buggy overtook me with two young men in it. They were in swimming trunks and wearing snorkel masks. As I looked on in amazement, they stopped at the edge of one of the lakes or large ponds and each jumped in and emerged with a couple of buckets filled with balls. The thundering noise occurred when they emptied the 'lake balls' into a 50 gallon oil drum on the back of the buggy. I considered this to be a fine example of the entrepreneurial spirit of the young men and the inaccuracy of the typical American club golfer.

The golf course in Nicosia, Cyprus, was divided by the 'Green Line' drawn between the Turkish and Greek sectors of that lovely country. Some of the semi-ruined houses running along the fairways were occupied by troops of the Swedish contingent in the United Nations Force In Cyprus (UNFICYP). They had made themselves very comfortable but could they drink? In one abode the walls were lined with empty beer cans as a form of alcoholic décor. It had a home made sauna as well and when it came time to liven up the steam a ladle of Schnapps or Acquavit or some other handy spirit was sprinkled onto the hot stones.

Drunkenness was then achieved by a process of osmosis and that last missed putt was soon forgotten.

I have been lucky enough to play some well-known and lesser-known courses in many parts of the world but like all golfers my favourite is my own – Ashridge in my case. It has history: Sir Henry Cotton was the Professional. It has drama: the thatched club house was burned down by a 'mad arsonist' in 1942, and it has a great layout with three starting points all of which can be viewed from the veranda of the modern clubhouse. In 1933 Walter Hagen beat Henry Cotton 2 and 1 here and four years later Henry went on to win the Open at Carnoustie while still the Professional at Ashridge. His woods are a feature of the bar. I feel fortunate to be a member of this club and only wish that my play could do it justice.

No doubt golfers across the globe feel the same about their own club. And why not!

HOLE 14

'Och Noo'

Par 4 Stroke Index 2
Are You Fixed?

Much of the enjoyment of golf is in the expectation: you can do better, you have had a lesson, you finished well last week or you just can't wait to try out that new pitching wedge that the Pro swears by. You set off from home with a spring in your step and goodwill to one and all. As the interpreter said to a German friend of mine on a business trip to China, 'Mr Sielemann, the sky is brue, the frowers are glowing, the birds are singing. In fact, Spling is just alound the corner.'

Surely, one of the great pleasures of golf is the people you meet. Well, nearly all the people. The fly in the ointment is, of course, THAT MAN whose golfing personality gets up everyone's nose. He is quite different from the club bore who can be tolerated (in small doses), but THAT MAN, and he is usually called Sydney, is to be avoided at all costs if both a steady handicap and a stable blood pressure are to be maintained.

Picture the scene. You have arrived at the club car park in eager anticipation of a friendly Sunday morning four-ball. As is the custom, you have made no previous playing arrangements and will be delighted to make up a four with whoever is available. Anticipation of a great day is high, the weather is perfect and the course is looking great. But, hang on, surely something is wrong? You can sense it. Old Harry, who is normally out of his Saab and on his way to the clubhouse before the turbo-charger has stopped turning is, for some obscure reason, buried under the bonnet. Bob, who is renowned for his aversion to practice and his game shows it, is chipping assiduously on the edge of the practice green. Your senses are alerted to danger but, as yet, you just can't quite make out what form it will take. In the clubhouse there is a strange atmosphere. More than the usual number of late starters are lingering over coffee and all the lavatories are occupied. In fact only two members are actually preparing to go out and play and they show more anxiety than enthusiasm.

Then it hits you … but, oh no, too late. Before you can dash into the Pro's shop to examine that £540 driver with graphite shaft and matt black finish, you hear those dreaded words that so many others have managed to avoid. 'You fixed, we need one more?'

As if by some process of osmosis your reluctant smile and hesitant nod of resigned acceptance travels around the clubhouse. Almost immediately Old Harry and Bob appear. Lavatories flush in dramatic unison and the occupants emerge energetically like moths escaping from their chrysalises. Empty coffee cups clatter into saucers, lockers bang open and conversation rises to its usual clamour. Yes, the club is returning to normal life. But for you and the other two penitents, all joy vanishes as you make your hesitant way to the start of your Sunday morning journey to Calvary, the first tee … and HIM.

Sydney is of course waiting there already, agitated by your tardy appearance. 'Come on, we don't want to be held up. Let's get on with it.' He has already decided partners; after all club stakes are worth winning and his encyclopaedic knowledge of all handicaps and the most recent adjustments ensures the playing balance is always in his favour. And so the game begins. Sydney knows all the rules and misses no opportunity to remind you of them. He lives and breathes etiquette and is a master of the withering glance and the huffy re-set if you have even a mild muscle spasm within 40 yards of him at address. He also has a complaint about every hole, continues to putt when it is given, knows the latest bar price increases to the nearest decimal point and has represented the County at rumour-mongering. All this could be tolerated, just, if only HE applied the same standards to his own behaviour … but he doesn't. No branch ever impedes his swing, bad lies are magically eased by a little downward pressure with the foot, stud scrapes follow his every move on the green and he's always in your peripheral vision when you are putting. What's more, HIS is the most smelly, badly behaved, flea ridden canine delinquent that you have ever come across in your whole life.

Now, now, calm down, it's getting to you. No matter how hard you try and keep control, exasperation affects every aspect of your finely tuned game and this unfortunately affords him the infuriating opportunity to tell you what you are doing wrong. Then as you fume, silently, the bugger sinks a 20 foot putt for a birdie and tells us this is the first he has had for weeks!

At last the game is over. You've lost, you've failed to break 100 for the first time in weeks, you have hurt your wrist and depleted your ball stock by three. But never mind, it's over, at long last it's over. Take consolation that HE is the victor and HE will be buying the drinks and you intend to order a very large one. But it's not to be for, try as you might, there is no way you or anyone else can manage to follow Sydney into the bar. You would need to take a sauna, be manicured and read two chapters of *War and Peace* to achieve this. He is a past master at arriving as the drinks are ordered, accepting a large Pimms (everyone else has a small beer) and leaving before it is his round.

Tell me, do you recognise THAT MAN? I'm sure every club has one. So what can be done to deter this pest who is even more of a threat to the enjoyment of golf than thatch on the greens or the dreaded shank? Well, there are three courses of action which can be considered: defence, counterattack or disinformation.

The first we have already touched upon. Like Old Harry and Bob, be ever alert to his potential presence and have an avoidance contingency plan to hand. If that doesn't work wheel out the ready excuse: 'yes I'd love to but I've got to have a word with the Pro about my new trolley' or 'I have to have a word with the Secretary.' If you can claim the onset of an upset tummy and at the same time contort your face in agony before rushing to the gents then so much the better. Once in you're safe because he will lose patience and hi-jack another victim.

Counterattack is, perhaps, the best form of defence and if done well is quite rewarding. With this ploy you do to HIM everything (and more) that HE has done to others but warn your playing partners first. Correct his grip, move about noisily at the address, stand on his line and, wonderfully effective, hit his dog with one off the heel. HE will never ask you again.

Disinformation is really the last resort. Tell new members what a delight he is to play with, start rumours with him and run a book on how quickly they get back to you, and try unleashing his dog while he is changing so that it runs loose on the 18th green as the Captain approaches.

But perhaps on reflection we are being too unkind and, in the best interests of the game and the good fellowship of your club it may be better when you next hear those dreaded words 'are you fixed?' to lie back, think of England and St George and sacrifice yourself for the sake of the game.

Oh, one other thing. Your name's not Sydney, is it?

HOLE 15

'Be Straight'

Par 5 Stroke Index 8

Psychometric Golf

One of the challenges about being promoted or changing your job is that you may have to move house, and if you're a golfer that means finding another club. With long waiting lists in many parts of the country that's not easy and in any case you will miss your old buddies and those familiar surroundings. Still, at least you will be able to re-circulate all your old jokes. The trouble is, even if you find a club with a vacancy, how are you going to find a proposer and, even more imponderable, how are you going to fare at the Committee's 'knife and fork' interview?

I'll let you into a secret. Club committees throughout the country are extremely concerned about the continued use of the subjective application Interview. They fear that in this litigious era their decisions could rebound on them, and no decent golf club wants to appear in the national press to justify its selection process. As a result there are moves afoot to get rid of the interview anachronism and move club golf into the 21st century by adopting the corporate practice of psychometric testing. The advantage is that the criterion is objective and, therefore, unchallengeable.

I have recently got hold of a draft copy of the Psychometric Test for Gentleman Membership of my club, which the committee has sent to the R&A for comment and approval. It is an interesting document and I suggest you try it for yourselves. Be honest and don't try to double guess the aim of each question. Remember, only tick the answer which most accurately represents your viewpoint.

Membership Application Test.

Questions   Answers (tick one answer only)

Q1. Which of the following occupations is **not** a proper profession?
a. Estate Agent.
b. Lawyer.
c. Plumber.
d. Accountant.

Q2. What do you think of the foursomes format? It is:-
a. The purest form of golf.
b. Half a game.
c. A trial of patience and manners.
d. Even worse when mixed.

Q3. If the Lady Captain enters the bar would you?
a. Stop telling that dirty story.
b. Change the ending.
c. Credit her with the original telling.

Q4. You are about to drive off from the first tee when the Captain and his four-ball arrives. Would you?
a. Drive off anyway.
b. Offer him the tee.
c. Consult your four-ball before offering the tee.
d. Tell him that trolleys are not allowed.

Q5. Would you recognise the Captain?
a. Oh yes.
b. No.
c. For a short period after the AGM.

Q6. Should the Seniors have reserved tee times?
a. Yes.
b. No.
c. Will they keep to them?
d. Will they remember them?

Q7. On what grounds would you suspect a player's handicap?
a. He consistently plays to it.
b. He always wins the Saturday roll-up but never enters competitions.
c. He repairs tine marks.
d. He has covers on his irons.

Q8. Should shorts be allowed?
a. Only with long socks.
b. With short or long socks.
c. With no socks.
d. Only by (some) ladies.

Q9. At the AGM would you?
a. Attend reluctantly
b. Sit at the front.
c. Hide in the crowd.
d. Stand at the back with a pint and make sarcastic remarks.

Q10. Should there be reserved parking in the car park?
a. Only for the President and the Club Captain.
b. For the Captain and 'Any Member'. This would be democratic.
c. Only for expensive cars.

Q11. What drink would you choose with Moroccan spiced lamb and glazed vegetables?
a. A Merlot.
b. A Sauternes.
c. An Egyptian Beaujolais.
d. Any proper Champagne.
e. A Coke.

Q12. What length of short putt should be given?
a. A putter's grip.
b. None.
c. Depends on whose it is.
d. My partner can decide.

Q13. Should Society players wear a jacket and tie for lunch?
a. Definitely.
b. Not on hot days.
c. Yes, providing the tie does not have a Windsor knot.
d. Societies should not have use of the dining room.

Q14. Should dogs be allowed on the course?
a. Yes, but proper ones.
b. Only if the owner's handicap is reduced by four on the day.
c. Only the Captain's (because it is better behaved than him).

Q15. How do you pronounce trousers?
a. Trowsers.
b. Trizers.
c. Tryzors
d. Trarzers.

Q 16. Should soup bowls be tilted away or towards the diner?
a. Away.
b. Towards.
c. To the side when dunking bread.

Q17. What is the correct reply to 'How do you do?'
a. How do you do.
b. Pleased to meet you.
c. Hi.
d. Like, great man, great.

Q18. When emerging from the shower should gentlemen wear their towel …
a. Around their waist.
b. Over their shoulder.
c. Or discard it.

Q19. What is smart/casual?
a. Blazer, flannels and tie.
b. Blazer, flannels with shirt collar worn inside the blazer.
c. As for above but shirt collar worn over the blazer collar.
c. None of the above but jeans somewhere.

Q20. Is your car …
a. British.
b. German, French or Scandinavian.
c. Japanese or Korean.
d. Other.

Q21. Who should laugh the loudest at the Captain's jokes at the Men's Dinner?
a. The Secretary.
b. The Pro.
c. The Members.
d. The Captain.

Q22. If a lady member stumbles upon you urinating in the woods, would you?
  a. Stop the flow if you could.
  b. Ask her to prove that she is a member.
  c. Smile proudly and apologise.
  d. Deny everything, and point out that you were merely practising the Harry Vardon overlapping grip.

Q23. How well do you know the Rules of Golf?
  a. Thoroughly.
  b. Well enough when it suits me.
  c. Ah, come on …

Q24. Should there be a television in the bar?
  a. No.
  b. God forbid.
  c. What?
  d. Only for rugger internationals and the Open.

Q25. Why do you want to join our club?
  a. It has huge snob appeal and will benefit my business.
  b. The friendliness and charm of the Committee truly reflect the public's and my own perception of the club and its membership.
  d. I don't, but I couldn't get in anywhere else.
  e. It's convenient to my home and a good test of golf.

Good, well that's it then. Remember there are no right or wrong answers but a statistical assessment of the trends of your selections will determine if you are the right sort. By the way, clean shoes and a reasonable handicap will help as well.

HOLE 16

'The Ridings'

Par 3 Stroke Index 14

Golf on Horseback

Apart from golf, polo is the only game that I know of that has a workable handicap system. I'm referring to polo played with a stick, a ball and a pony and not to that exhausting, mostly under-water affair played mainly by Eastern Europeans. It is also a game where ladies can compete on equal terms with men although the horse does help a bit. It is well worth watching though and is very skilful.

Just down the road from our barracks in Kenya in the 1960s was the Kenyatta Polo Club which, to be truthful, had seen better times. The owner had two charming but muscular daughters, both of whom were rumoured to be capable of hitting a 'backhander under the dock,' the dock being the technical term for the bony stump left after a horse's tail has been cropped. In the polo world, apparently, such a stroke requires great horsemanship and considerable strength, and believe me they had both in abundance. We officers who could ride a little were always welcome to exercise the ponies and try our luck at the game, and it cost us nothing. It was also a good way for Mum and Dad, I imagine, to put their girls in the shop window, or am I being unkind?

I enjoyed the sport and even considered getting a pony of my own. On the grapevine I heard that a Kenya Regiment officer in Lanet, a small outpost near Nakuru, was selling one so I gave him a call and went to have a look at it. It seemed to be a very handy pony as it was trotted around by a smart African syce, or groom as we know it, but when haggling over the price I asked the owner some questions on feeding and veterinary costs and the salary of a groom.

'Forget about the latter,' said the owner, 'the price includes the syce for a year.' So, I was about to buy a horse and a man as well. For once I showed some common sense and decided to stick with the freebie riding and the company of the lovely, but rather large ladies-in-waiting.

My short polo career came to an end in Malta which I visited to meet up with some friends who were stationed there. I travelled courtesy of the RAF Indulgence System which entitled servicemen to travel free on service aircraft providing they guaranteed to get themselves back if a return flight was unavailable. My journey took me from Nairobi to Aden where I stayed for a couple of days with a buddy, then on to Malta via RAF El Adem in Libya, Benghazi and Tripoli. The last three stages were in a twin-engine Royal Navy Sea Devon whose crew of two appeared to be 'in their cups' for most of the journey. As a result of some dodgy food and water I had also managed to pick up a combination of Aden Gut, 'Gyppy' Tummy and Malta Dog and demonstrated, as the navigator so delicately pointed out to me, that I 'could shit through the eye of a needle.'

My three week stay on the lovely George Cross Island was great fun, lots of parties, good food and great swimming and sunning in the Officers' Lido where one day I chanced to see some nuns bathing on the opposite side of the little bay. They were wearing flowing, white, semi-diaphanous gowns which billowed out around them as they made their stately way into deeper water. Like an armada of giant jellyfish they drifted to and fro, enjoying the warm water and possibly sampling passing algae, until their time was up. Then, in a paroxysm of violent effort hampered all the way by their outfits, they achieved a mass beach landing and made their way like sodden brides to their bus. It was very bizarre.

One morning I had the opportunity to help exercise some polo ponies and, by a miracle, showed that I could get my animal to change its leading leg at a canter. In truth it was more down to the horse than me. Anyway, this was spotted and I was invited to play on the polo ground near Valetta on the following Saturday. In borrowed kit and never having played a proper chukka before, I decided on a bit of practice on the wooden horse in the training facility. My confidence took a blow when I fell off, twice.

Polo on the Maidan in Malta was a much smarter do than anything offered by the Kenyatta Club. There were a couple of hundred specta-tors, and most of the players seemed to be either high ranking Army and Navy officers, members of the local aristocracy, or beautiful rose cheeked English girls who looked marvellous in their tight jodhpurs.

Later, though, through those well-bred, Home Counties lips emerged some of the foulest language that I have ever heard. Polo brought out the worst in them.

I didn't play straightaway but was ordered by a colonel, who seemed to be in charge, to be the umpire; tricky this as I didn't really know the rules.

'No problem,' he said, 'you'll soon pick them up, and anyway we'll help.' Thus it was that I found myself sitting in the middle of the polo field, on a clapped out ex-polo pony, with a double rein which I'd never used before, a helmet which was too big for me, a crop with a whistle on one end, and a satchel full of balls around my neck, and matters got worse. Over the next fifteen minutes I found myself totally out of my depth as the eight players thundered around, raising huge amounts of dust, and screaming obscenities at each other.

'Keep out of my bloody f***ing way Hugo, you bastard,' or, 'you can't ride me off like that, you little s**t.' And this from the young ladies.

My role as I understood it was to adjudicate and keep order but there were two issues preventing this. First I didn't have a clue what to do and second, I couldn't get my horse to move faster than a slow walk. I was like a Buddhist Stupa set serenely in the Centre of the Universe as the problems of the world revolved around me at the gallop; except that I was not serene.

'Eighty yarder,' or something like that, screamed the colonel and I flapped my legs ever harder to force my reluctant nag to the spot he indicated. 'For Christ's sake hurry up,' he roared as Dobbin and I shambled slowly in his direction.

His face by now was puce with rage so I decided on a desperate measure. Knowing that I was incapable of cantering over, wheeling in a tight turn, and dropping a ball for play to continue, I reached into my satchel and hurled a ball over arm towards him. This, I later found out, was the equivalent of slurping tea out of a saucer at the Queen's Garden Party or standing on the neck of a downed pheasant to drown it in a puddle rather than face ringing its neck. Somehow I knew that I was unlikely to be part of the polo set for very much longer.

The end was ignominious, but rather heroic in a way. As I was trying to regain my composure a ball flashed past me and I looked round to see both teams pursuing it at a full gallop accompanied by a cacophony of obscenities and swirling sticks – and here, dear, was I, slap bang in the way. I didn't pray but an Act of God intervened, for my steed, which until now had been showing all the signs of equine dementia, remembered its past glories. It whinnied, looked at the ball, pricked up its ears and, with a loud fart, dashed off in pursuit.

You will understand that I had no choice in the matter, so with my helmet over my eyes, my double rein and whistle uncomfortable in my sweaty grasp, and my satchel of balls bouncing out of control, I led the charge of the 'heavy brigade' for the entire length of the field and on, and on.

I was retired from my duties shortly afterwards, but I had a lot of drinks bought for me that evening by my non-polo playing friends who found it all highly amusing. I never played again.

HOLE 17

'Home'

Par 5 Stroke Index 6

Arms and the Man

After recovering from the wounds that I had sustained in the battle of the Khyber Pass in 1876 I considered my future in the army. My Regiment, the 71st Highland Light Infantry, had been entirely decimated in that sad action and the thought of continuing my career without the many chums that I had served with for years was not an attractive proposition. Besides which, following the Cardwell Reforms of '71 banning the purchase of promotion, the chance of further advancement was unlikely. As a colleague put it, 'It is a strange world, Major McDonald, when ability appears to outweigh money and connections.' So it was that I made the decision to return to Scotland and concentrate on the care of my estates.

For years now these had been the responsibility of my younger brother, a rather dull young man whose main interest in life, indeed his only interest, was cooking, of all things, God! No hunting, shooting, fishing or worse, no golf, he seemed to spend most of his day shredding and frying beef and moulding the result into a pastry-less pie of sorts. Something that no gentleman would be seen eating. He had also allowed much of my estate to be taken over by tenant farmers and crofters who were allowed to scratch a living off the land in exchange for a meagre rent. A useful income, I admit, but entirely unnecessary, and I made this abundantly clear to Ronald when I returned to my ancestral castle. Scraggy bovids were everywhere and you could hardly walk or ride a dozen miles or so before stumbling on a pitiful bothy inhabited by gormless men and women and hordes of filthy children. 'This is not what Scotland is all about,' I thought, so I cancelled their tenancies with immediate effect but, benevolently, gave them two weeks to move off my land.

Ronald didn't agree with this of course and said that he was not prepared to continue in this 'stultifying backwater' as he put it, saying that he would emigrate to America and start up a chain of fast food outlets. I had no idea what he was talking about.

'You can try any madcap scheme you want, Ronald, but when it fails because people won't want to rush in and guzzle your pies instead of partaking in a leisurely and civilised repast there will always be a place for you here.' Although the man was an ass he was, after all, my brother and I had no wish to abandon him to his ridiculous pipe dreams. And so we parted: he to his 'squat and gobbles' and me to the things that really mattered, like shooting and golf.

Over the following years the sporting value of my land increased. It became a mecca of country pursuits for a good number of friends and the local gentry but it was the golf course that I became most proud of. Starting with six holes based on the memorable little links where I had shared the Khyber Cup with poor old Hook-Ballantyne, I developed it into a very nice venue with some truly magnificent holes and stunning views. I named it The Ballantyne after Sandy who, the day after that heroic match, was blown into smithereens when he unfortunately fell into the barrel of a siege mortar just before it was fired. In a way though, he played his part, or rather bits of him did, in weakening the ramparts of the Afridi fort we were engaging at the time.

I, of course, continued to play golf even though I was down to one arm, luckily the left one. As all golfers know it is the leading arm that controls the shot and produces most of the power. The other provides some stability and control but I found that my disability could be overcome by strengthening the muscles in my remaining limb through strenuous exercises designed around my daily activities. For a start I increased the weight of my whiskey and brandy glasses by only drinking doubles and trebles and more of them. I had brought my bearer Mohan back with me and, good servant that he was, he soon picked up the routine. I also increased their apparent weight by holding the glass at full arm extension to my left and parallel to the ground and slowly swinging it through a ninety degree arc ahead of me before bringing it to my mouth to sup. I made no exceptions to this routine even on social occasions and I always found that the lady or gentleman sitting *ad sinistram* was most accommodating about this manoeuvre. But it mattered little as, in time, the number of invitations I received to dine inexplicably declined.

I also walked everywhere with my arm locked in a perpendicular fashion above my head while holding a small cannon ball. After a few weeks I could conduct my business with my arm in this position for two or three hours at a time thus benefiting immensely the muscles of the sub-scapularis and trapezius. I relaxed the muscle afterwards by repeated saluting, the longest way up and the shortest way down. I also found it important to strengthen the grip in my hand and found the best way to do this was to clench and unclench a turnip until it disintegrated. Mohan was always in attendance with spares when required and carefully cleaned up the pulp which I had deposited. I freely admit that some ladies glanced askance if this occurred in their drawing room but I am sure that they appreciated that there was a good reason for this. You will not be surprised that after a few months I found these exercises, conducted routinely throughout the day, improved my game immeasurably and I recommend them to fully armed golfers wholeheartedly.

And so the years passed pleasantly enough, marked by the seasons for hooking salmon and trout and slaughtering deer, grouse and pheasants. Throughout this time The Ballantyne matured into a wonderful course. So much so that one day I was surprised to be visited by Mr James Braid, a well-known professional who had just won the first of five Open Championships. He had heard of my course and being interested in design asked if he could perhaps play a round with me. He was a nice man though not the sort that I would normally associate or play with but I made an exception in this case. After the first hole I asked him to what did he attribute his great length off the tee and I will always remember his reply, 'A slow backswing and keep your jacket fastened.'

I was much heartened by his impression of the course and learned something from the tips he gave me: comfortable footwear whether it be a good pair of boots with nails for the winter or lighter rubber soled boots for the summer. He also recommended carrying a piece of billiard chalk to smear on the face of my woods on a wet day and to carry a 'small tin of Vaseline as may be bought for a penny' to grease my iron clubs thus preventing an overnight coating of rust. He showed much interest in my strengthening exercises but I remained impassive when he said that a successful golfer's habits must be regular and he must refrain from excessive drinking, smoking and short hours of sleep. A little practice as well, he advised, does no harm even if it involves hitting a few pitching shots with balls made out of paper off a door mat, whatever that is.

At the conclusion of our round he commended me on my one-armed play but said that my putting could be improved by a lighter putter like the one he had just been introduced to. It was made of a new material called aluminium. I nodded but was not convinced. I was somewhat relieved when he said that he could not stay for dinner but as he settled himself in his brougham before journeying to the railway station he remarked, 'I was chatting to Walter Travis, the US Amateur Champion at the Open last month and said that I planned to visit your course, Major McDonald.' Travis had said, 'How strange, I met a MacDonald or McDonald in Illinois a few weeks back who owned a number of neat little restaurants across the state serving mainly fried beef in a bun. Apparently, the idea was going well and he asked if I would be interested in going into business with him. I thought about it, but decided there was no future there.'

'Any relation?' asked Braid. I shook my head and thought that Travis was obviously as good a business man as he was a golfer.

I watched Braid as he was driven out of sight and then, with Mohan behind me with a tray of turnips and a bottle of brandy, I walked slowly back to my castle with my arm held stiffly above my head.

HOLE 18

'Nearly There'

Par 4 Stroke Index 10

Last Post

Some years back the committee of my Golfing Society met at the very pleasant Bognor Regis club for a round of golf, a very good lunch and, if we had time afterwards, a short meeting to discuss the business of the Society. As we gathered in the bar before lunch we were joined by a sprightly, silver haired gentleman who introduced himself as a previous member of our Society. We, of course, invited him to lunch and great company he was too. We were astounded when he mentioned that he was one hundred years old and played 18 holes twice a week. I am pretty sure that by now he has climbed the long fairway to paradise but then he was living proof that alcoholic lunches and golf are good for longevity. Perhaps the former should be tempered with caution but the health giving qualities of the great game are undeniable.

I now only play in the rarefied atmosphere of the Seniors' Section of my club. You qualify for that at the age of sixty and the production of a £5 note for your annual subscription. This assures you of a genial twice a week gathering, a monthly medal, weekly opportunities to play in matches against other clubs at a very low fee, and some excellent dinners and other convivial gatherings with like-minded souls. Having enthused thus, I put off joining for about ten years believing that I could still compete with the younger members at the weekend roll-ups (wrong) and that joining the Seniors would hasten my deterioration into senility (wrong, but …) and that I would begin secreting that slightly musty odour that surrounds many old folk (you don't know that unless others tell you). Wives of mature gentlemen are very good though at keeping us on the straight and narrow regarding personal hygiene as well as reminding us to keep our mouths closed except when talking or eating. An early sign of 'losing it' is, apparently, standing silently, slightly hunched with a slack mouth; a normal stance when considering a tricky putt I say.

In my club Seniors' handicaps range from lowish to quite high and you can be drawn to play with or against anyone on our weekly play days. In the summer we tee off at 12.45 and in the winter an hour earlier. Wonderful, no more getting up early in all weathers and always plenty of time for a leisurely breakfast and a detailed read of the morning papers. Seniors know all, have views on everything and can provide the answers to all the world's problems; so keeping up with current affairs is essential if you want to be part of this happy band. The hour spent consuming the tea cakes that the losers buy, witnesses some of the most erudite discussions ever experienced by mankind. However, because the standard of our hearing is not as acute as it was a few years back misunderstandings can and do occur.

'Careful, the tea's hot Charlie' … 'What, who shot him then?'

The decline in awareness can be seen in other ways as well. Our team was short of two players in a home match because they had travelled to our opponent's club. Sadly, one was the Fixtures Secretary!

Having said this there is nothing antiquated about the way we play the game. First we play quickly; none of this professional nonsense of lining up putts from all angles or consulting the distance card at every shot. Time is limited for us so we get on with it. So too, there is no more faithful customer of the Professional's shop than a Senior. All boast the latest trolleys and bags, the finest clubs and the most accurate range-finders. The fact that none of these work for us consistently is neither here nor there. Ah well, hope springs eternal. 'He hits the ball out of sight' is no accurate commentary on a partner's power play but more about the other's failing eyesight. Seniors also tend to be distracted by many things that they can't control; rheumy eyes, forgetting the number of shots played, whether you get a stroke on a particular hole or not and, of course, by frequent trips into the tree-line to relieve a weakening bladder.

Indeed, although there is seldom a need to reserve a tee time in my club I occasionally consider that booking a slot for a urinal would be a wise move. I well remember having a pee alongside a distinguished but very skinny retired judge who stood naked, white, sagging and counting slowly as he waited for the cursory old man's meagre flow to commence. 'One, two, three,' perhaps this was a new relief for prostate sufferers, I thought but no, 'four, five, you know,' he said turning to me, 'I had five pars today.' And in a couple of shakes he was off.

But the greatest benefit of being a senior is the medical advice that is freely available whether you want it or not. Seniors are a walking Gray's Anatomy and proud of it and there is not a disease or problem that someone in the Seniors has not experienced. It is seldom that a four ball can muster eight natural hips or knees, four unassisted hearts or four working prostates.

At the age of 80 you move into the company of the Super Seniors who play nine holes whenever and wherever they want to. This move is not compulsory. Some SSs have their own buggies and specially adapted cars to load them into. It is a privileged sight to see three or four of these wrinkly specimens setting off in their carts like some geriatric formation team. They are entitled as well to stand vacantly with their mouths open without fear of rebuke.

So, as we see, there are various ways to enter the Senior fraternity but, unfortunately, only one way out. The club flag at half-mast signals to the aspiring member of the club that a vacancy is about to be announced and it also records that another old golfer has just faded away, much like his drives over the past few years I could add. Then it's the memorial service and a jolly good wake with plenty of grog to remember him by. I might make the Super Seniors soon and I have decided that when I have run out of balls, excuses and oxygen I would like my ashes scattered on the 18th where my shots have also been scattered so pleasurably over many years.

Hereafterthought

The Paradise Golf Club

Our course is great and, wow, the view,
        the weather's fine, the greens are true.

Our drives are straight and no one slices,
        in fact we are devoid of vices.

Approach shots always hit the pin
        and every putt goes dead straight in.

But then again it's not the same
        as playing a truly testing game.

You never win or lose a match
        'cos everyone is bloody scratch.

So when I can I creep below
        and play with mates from long ago.

The rough is up, it's stinking hot
        and anyone can duff a shot.

With demons present on our back
        we top and hook and slice and hack.

The lies are poor, the greens have thatch
        But, goodness, it's a proper match.

So swear and drink and fornicate
        for golf's not golf through the Pearly Gate.